GO
INTO
ALL
THE
WORLD

Embracing the Mission Mandate
of God's Covenant

GO
INTO
ALL
THE
WORLD

Daniel Holstege

REFORMED
FREE PUBLISHING
ASSOCIATION
Jenison, Michigan

© 2025 Reformed Free Publishing Association
All rights reserved.

Printed in the United States of America.

No part of this publication may be reproduced, stored in a retrieval system, or transmitted in any form or by any means—electronic, mechanical, photocopying, recording, or otherwise—without the prior written permission of the publisher. The only exception is brief quotations in reviews.

Scripture cited is taken from the King James (Authorized) Version. Italics in Scripture quotations reflect the author's emphasis.

Cover design by Erika Kiel
Interior design by Katherine Lloyd, The DESK

Reformed Free Publishing Association
1894 Georgetown Center Drive
Jenison, Michigan 49428
616-457-5970
mail@rfpa.org
www.rfpa.org

ISBN: 9781736815496
Ebook ISBN: 9798987161401
LCCN: 2025939836

*To Leah, beloved wife and mother,
who has always filled our home with goodness
and supported her husband in his ministry,
even when the God of the covenant sent us
faraway to the islands of the sea.
I thank my God for you.*

CONTENTS

ACKNOWLEDGEMENTS xi

INTRODUCTION 1
   A Little Background 1
   Why This Book? 5
   What's the Plan? 9

1 BIBLICAL OVERVIEW: ADAM TO NOAH 13
   The Covenant in the Beginning 13
   The Covenant and the Fall 15
   The Covenant and the Flood 19

2 BIBLICAL OVERVIEW: ABRAHAM TO CHRIST 23
   Abraham and His Seed 23
   A Father of Many Nations 25
   The Nations to Flow into Mount Zion 29
   A Savior for All Nations, Tribes, and Tongues 31
   Go into All the World 34

3 GOD'S ETERNAL COUNSEL, COVENANT,
   AND MISSIONS 37
   As My Father Sent Me into the World… 37
   God's Will to Reveal His Covenant by Establishing
   a Covenant with Us through Christ 41
   …Even So Do I Send You into the World 45

4 GOD'S TWO WAYS OF ESTABLISHING HIS COVENANT ... 49
   Two Truths 50
   The Covenant with Believers and Their Seed in Israel 52

    The Enlargement of the Covenant in All the World......... 54
    Our Covenantal Mission Mandate 57
    In Summary 60

5 A CULTURE FOR MISSIONS IN THE COVENANTAL
    COMMUNITY... 63
    Creating a Culture for Missions 64
    A Culture for Teaching the Children of Believers.......... 66
    A Culture for Missions in Our Homes....................... 68
    A Culture for Missions in Our Schools...................... 73
    A Culture for Missions in Our Churches 78

6 GO INTO ALL THE WORLD, BUT BE YE SEPARATE!......... 83
    Israel in the Midst of the Nations 85
    Come Out, Then Go In!.. 87
    Getting Practical and Concrete.............................. 91

7 GO INTO ALL THE WORLD, BUT FEED MY SHEEP!......... 99
    An Ingrown Church.. 100
    The Gift of Missionaries 104
    The Missionary in the World................................. 106

8 FINDING MOTIVATION TO EVANGELIZE FROM
    GOD'S COVENANT 115
    Why the Lack of Motivation? 116
    How Does the Covenant Motivate Us to Witness?........ 120
    Bringing Outsiders into the Covenantal Community..... 123

9 EVANGELIZING IN HOPE OF THE FINAL PERFECTION
    OF GOD'S COVENANT.. 129

Appendix 1 THE GREAT COMMISSION 137
Appendix 2 ECHOING THE WORD 145
            SCRIPTURE INDEX 153

ACKNOWLEDGEMENTS

Before this book was written, a much rougher version of its content was published as a series of articles while I was doing mission work in the Philippines. A good friend who was working for the RFPA at the time, Alex Kalsbeek, encouraged me to write on the relationship between the covenant and missions. I agreed that it was a subject worthy of closer examination, and I started thinking about it. I wrote some articles for the "Go Ye into All the World" rubric in the *Standard Bearer*. Soon after finishing those articles, I decided to attempt putting them into book form. That proved to be more difficult and time consuming than I anticipated. But it was rewarding work.

This is the first book I have written. I was struck by how many people work behind the scenes in the publication of a book! Only one person's name ends up on the cover as the author. But before the book sees the light of day, many others help him develop and refine his writing and offer suggestions for enhancing the book. I am grateful to all of you at the RFPA who have supported my work and expressed excitement about getting this book published.

Several people read the manuscript in its various stages of development. I consider Cory Griess and Jonathan Mahtani, two of my brothers in the ministry, to be kindred spirits when it comes to thinking about missions. I thank you both for taking the time to read and critique my manuscript in one of its early stages. You not only offered encouragement, but also suggestions for improvement. I believe I implemented most if not all of your suggestions.

I would also like to express appreciation to a few men from denominations other than my own who read and endorsed my book: Paul Murphy (United Reformed Churches in North America), Eric Onderwater (Canadian and American Reformed Churches), and Tim Bergsma (Free Reformed Churches of North America). Though we may disagree about the definition of God's covenant and its members, I have discovered through conversations with you or through reading your writings that we all agree on the need to inspire our churches to increased focus and action in the evangelizing of the lost. We all agree that God will extend his covenant both to the children of believers *and* to all that are afar off, even as many as the Lord our God shall call.

I gratefully acknowledge that the Lord has used many different people to teach, inspire, support, or partner with me in missions, including Jason Kortering, Bill Bruinsma, Barry Gritters, Daniel Kleyn, Richard Smit, Vernon Ibe, and others; including Reformed believers in the Philippines and United States who are enthusiastic about evangelism. I thank God for my family and friends who have been so supportive of my mission work and writing, especially my wife Leah, who is always a tremendous helper and listener. But most of all, I acknowledge my Lord Jesus himself who has all authority in heaven and on earth, for he is the one who spoke to my heart through the words of his great commission. May he speak those words to your heart too.

—Daniel Holstege

INTRODUCTION

In this last age, God is fulfilling his promise to Abraham by establishing his covenant with all the families of the earth through the mission enterprise of his church, but also with the children of those who believe the gospel in the lines of continuing generations. This last part we have understood well in the Reformed tradition. But the first part has too often been neglected or ignored. My hope and prayer with this book is to contribute something positive in the development of our thinking and practice when it comes to the covenant of grace and our mission to the nations.

This is certainly not the first contribution of its kind. Others within my own theological tradition have already written and spoken about covenant and missions, and I owe much of my own growth in this area to the wisdom and insight God has given them. I hope that this book will build on what they have taught, advance our understanding of this subject somewhat, and encourage us to think more deeply and practically about the realities and callings that are discussed here.

A Little Background

I was born into a line of believers in Christ in which God had been establishing his covenant for many generations. I was raised by Christian parents who both grew up in the covenantal community as manifested in the Protestant Reformed

Churches in America (PRCA). They, too, were raised by Christian parents who grew up in either the Protestant Reformed or Christian Reformed churches.

My parents, like theirs before them, believed that infants of believers "are included in the covenant and church of God."[1] Therefore, they brought me as an infant to be baptized as a sign of the covenant that God established with me, in the Southeast Protestant Reformed Church in Grand Rapids, Michigan. They brought me to church and sent me to catechism throughout my childhood, so I came under the preaching of the gospel and came to know the God who gave his Son to die for my sins. They sent me to good Christian schools from kindergarten through high school, so I learned how to view the world and life from a Christian perspective.

When I was eighteen, I stood up in the same church in which I was baptized and publicly confessed my faith. I ate the bread of the Lord's supper and drank the wine, a sign and seal of the "blood of the new testament," the blood of the covenant, which Jesus shed for me and for many for the remission of our sins (Matt. 26:28; Mark 14:24).

I was taught growing up that God establishes his covenant with believers and their seed in their generations within the church. That rang true to my experience too. But I was not taught in a clear or emphatic way that God also establishes his covenant with people outside the church. I do not mean that people in our churches did not believe that. They certainly did. I heard it preached from Protestant Reformed pulpits and read it in Protestant Reformed literature. But the purpose of God to

---

[1] Heidelberg Catechism Q&A 74, in *The Confessions and Church Order of the Protestant Reformed Churches* (Grandville, MI: Protestant Reformed Churches in America, 2005), 111.

INTRODUCTION

bestow the mercies of his covenant on the elect who are still in the heathen world was not so emphasized as to instill a firm conviction about the urgency of missions or to produce the outpouring of energy and action that such a conviction calls for. I became aware of that urgency only gradually, especially while I was in seminary, through the teaching and writing of men who saw that lack and sought to remedy it.

When the Lord called me to pursue the ministry at the age of nineteen, I do not remember feeling a burden for those still lost in unbelief, but only a calling to be a pastor of a local church. That was daunting enough to me at the time. But during my seminary years, I became convinced more and more that the call to the ministry of the gospel is never merely a call to be a pastor of a church but always includes the call to do the work of an evangelist (Eph. 4:11; 2 Tim. 4:5).

I was surrounded by professors and students who showed a deep interest in missions. In September 2008, I attended an instructive conference on missions featuring several Protestant Reformed speakers, sponsored by the Domestic Mission Committee of my denomination. In January 2009, my fellow seminary students and I received the privilege of traveling with one of our professors to Westminster Seminary California for a very inspiring conference on what it means to be "missional and Reformed."[2] All of this goaded me to more focused attention on missions and evangelism.

So when I entered the ministry in 2010, I was eager to promote and engage in church evangelism. Whereas my conviction

---

[2] You can still listen to the speeches on their website at www.wscal.edu/resource-category/annual-conference/. Look for the six speeches from the January 2009 conference, "Missional and Reformed: Reaching the Lost and Teaching the Reached."

concerning the catechizing and education of the children of the covenant never waned, my conviction concerning outreach grew stronger. In my first congregation, one of the things we did was hold "witnessing workshops" in the summertime in which we attempted to instruct and encourage our members in their personal witnessing to their neighbors.

But in 2016, the Lord called me to preach the gospel in what to me, as an American, was one of "earth's remotest regions." I could not resist his call. The Lord gave me an eagerness to go and a wife who was willing and able to support me in that work. For the next eight months, we prepared to move around the world to the Philippines. For about five years, I had the joy of proclaiming Christ and witnessing God's establishment of his covenant with people of a nation and culture very different from my own. It gave new meaning to certain beloved psalms:

> The ends of all the earth shall hear
> And turn unto the Lord in fear;
> All kindreds of the earth shall own
> and worship him as God alone.
> All earth to him her homage brings,
> The Lord of lords, the King of kings.[3]

> O God, to us show mercy
> And bless us in thy grace;
> Cause thou to shine upon us
> The brightness of thy face;

---

[3] No. 49:1, in *The Psalter with Doctrinal Standards, Liturgy, Church Order, and Added Chorale Section*, reprinted and revised edition of the 1912 United Presbyterian *Psalter* (Grand Rapids, MI: Eerdmans, 1927; rev. ed. 1995).

INTRODUCTION

> That so thy way most holy
> On earth may soon be known,
> And unto every people
> Thy saving grace be shown.[4]
>
> Christ shall have dominion
> Over land and sea,
> Earth's remotest regions
> Shall his empire be;
> They that wilds inhabit
> Shall their worship bring,
> Kings shall render tribute,
> Nations serve our King.[5]

Why This Book?

Why write a book on covenant and missions? I wrote this book out of the conviction that we need a more developed and balanced understanding of the ways and places where God establishes his covenant in this last age. I wrote not because no one else has written or spoken on this subject before. But I wrote in order to carry forward and shout from the housetops what others have written and spoken. I wrote not because I think we conservative Reformed folk have utterly failed in our mission to the nations by devoting ourselves instead to the rearing of our own children. As I indicated above, I am deeply grateful to God for the Christian upbringing I received as a child of believers within God's covenant. But I wrote because I believe many of us Reformed believers still need to grow in

---
4 No. 176:1, in *The Psalter*.
5 No. 200:1, in *The Psalter*.

our understanding and practice of missions—local, domestic, and foreign—and need to see that this precious truth of the covenant that we tend to associate with us and our children is actually much bigger.

I do not know who will read this book. You might be a member of the same churches as I am, or a member of another Reformed denomination, or a Christian from outside the Reformed camp. I hope all of the above will read this book. I want you to know from the outset that my purpose in this book is not to refute the idea popular in Reformed circles that the covenant is a pact or agreement that God establishes with all the children of believers and all who hear the gospel on a mission field, in which he promises eternal life to them all, on the condition that they repent and believe. I simply state here my view that God promises salvation only to the elect.

God promises to save whoever believes in Christ crucified. He doesn't promise to save *all who hear* on the condition that they believe in Christ. But he promises to save *all who believe* in Christ. The elect are the only ones who come to faith in Christ (Acts 13:48). Therefore, it is clear: God promises salvation to the elect alone and gives that salvation to the elect alone.

That being said, God calls us to *preach* that promise of the gospel, together with the command to repent and believe, in all nations and to all persons without distinction because he has his people all throughout the earth.[6] We cannot limit our preaching to the elect because we do not know who is elect and who is not. What we do know is that God will save his elect

---

6 Canons of Dordt 2, article 5, in Philip Schaff, ed., *The Creeds of Christendom with a History and Critical Notes*, 6th ed., 3 vols. (New York: Harper and Row, 1931; repr., Grand Rapids, MI: Baker Books, 2007), 3:586.

INTRODUCTION

in all the world by faith in Christ, which he will work in them through the preaching of the gospel. So we must preach the gospel to all. But the purpose of this book is not to go deeper into that matter.

Nor is it the purpose of this book to take aim at the error of those Christians who think we ought not to baptize infants of believers until they grow up and come to a conscious faith in Christ. I only state my Reformed conviction that since God promises to establish his covenant with believers and their seed in their generations, we ought to baptize our children because they, as well as us adults, are members of the covenant (Gen. 17:7; Acts 2:39). There are many Baptist megachurches today with thousands of members and great passion to reach the masses, evangelize the cities, and win souls for Christ. We in Reformed circles must have just as great zeal to teach all nations, baptize the adult converts whom God saves through our mission work, and call sinners to Christ.

But we must never neglect to baptize the children of those adult converts too, catechize them diligently in the truths of Scripture, and teach them the Christian life. A church might become a megachurch by gathering under one roof or into several campuses many thousands of people who are disillusioned with their denominations or looking for some kind of spiritual experience. But it seems to me that if a church does not urge parents to bring their children to Jesus through baptism, to put them through a solid program of catechetical instruction, and to educate them in a good Christian school, such a church is unlikely to have a long lifespan.

But my purpose in this book is not to dismantle the viewpoint behind that kind of church. Many others have written books that tackle those matters. Rather, I hope to awaken

Reformed people to the truth that God's purpose is to establish his covenant not only with us and our elect children after us, but also with his people who are still lost in unbelief together with their elect children after them. My hope is that the heightened awareness of this will stir us up to greater evangelistic endeavors.

I also hope to demonstrate that although our zeal for missions certainly has ebbed and flowed in the Reformed community through history (isn't that true in every church?), that does not mean our doctrine of the covenant precludes a vision for local and world mission. Since the covenant is a doctrine of the Bible and missions is a calling from the Bible, it is impossible for there to be any conflict of interest between them. We just need to understand all of what the Bible teaches about them.

Before we go on, then, let me give a short, Bible-based definition of these two ideas of the covenant and missions. The covenant of grace, according to the whole testimony of the Holy Scriptures, is the everlasting relationship of well-structured friendship and fellowship between God and his people in Christ. God remains above us in this relationship. He is our majestic Creator and King, though he condescends to us in the person of the Son to redeem us from our sins and, by the operation of the Holy Spirit, to draw us into his loving arms. He is a Father to us. We remain under God in this relationship. We are his lowly creatures and subjects, though we move toward him in love and enjoy sweet communion with him by faith. We are his children. The covenant in its essence is this beautiful bond of well-ordered fellowship, life, and love between God and his elect people (Gen. 17:7; Ex. 29:45–46; Ps. 25:14; Isa. 41:8; Jer. 31:31–34; Ezek. 16:8; Matt. 26:28; 2 Cor. 6:16–18; Gal. 3:15–17; Rev. 21:3).

INTRODUCTION

What about missions? Missions is the work of God in Christ, in this last age of history, in which he calls his church to go out into the world to preach the gospel of salvation, leave a witness in all nations, baptize believers and their seed, and train converts to follow Christ. In missions, God in Christ gathers to himself all whom he ordained to eternal life before the foundation of the world and redeemed by the blood of the cross out of all nations, tribes, and tongues. In missions, God in Christ converts heathen idolaters to a saving faith in Jesus Christ and builds his church in all the world to the glory of his name. In missions, God in Christ does all this through those men whom he sends to preach, baptize, and teach the Scriptures. In addition, Christ calls all believers to join in this great work by confessing him before men and sounding out the gospel we hear in church to our neighbors in our daily lives. That is what I understand by "missions" (Matt. 16:18; 24:14; 28:19; Mark 16:15; Luke 12:8; Acts 26:17–18; Rom. 10:15; 1 Thess. 1:8).

I think my doctrinal assumptions and practical purposes are unique and make this book different from other books written on covenant and missions by authors who have a different view of the covenant.[7]

What's the Plan?

In the first two chapters of the book, I will set forth the big picture of what the Bible teaches about God's covenantal purposes as they relate to our mission to the nations. This overview of God's progressive revelation concerning his covenant will show

---

7 For example, Paul Wells, Peter A Lillback, and Henk Stoker, eds., *A Covenantal Vision for Global Mission* (Phillipsburg, NJ: P & R Publishing, 2020).

the particular and universal aspects of his eternal plan. I will begin in the beginning, scan the history of the Old Testament, and then look at the teaching of Jesus and his apostles in the New Testament.

In chapter 3, I will look back into eternity through the Scriptures at God's decree of the covenant, which arises out of God's own covenantal life and which is the fountainhead of our mission mandate to all nations. In this section, I will present what is known in Reformed theology as the *pactum salutis* (covenant of redemption) and what I believe to be a better understanding of the covenant of God within the Trinity. I will then show the connection between that eternal covenant and missions.

In chapter 4, I will turn your attention to the truth that God in the new dispensation has opened his covenant to all nations and establishes his covenant in two ways. I will show that in the old dispensation, God chose Israel from among the nations and established his covenant with believers and their seed almost exclusively in Israel. But in the new dispensation, with the death of the Messiah and outpouring of the Spirit on Pentecost, God has opened his covenant to all the nations and establishes his covenant with all who believe the gospel that he sends forth, together with their children. He continues to establish his covenant in the lines of the generations of believers. But now he also extends his covenant among the nations by sending his covenantal people to gather the covenantal people who are still lost. In our churches, then, we need to develop and foster a culture for missions as well as a culture that focuses on the children of believers.

Then in chapters 5 through 7, I will focus on our calling as the covenantal people to be witnesses of our God and Savior in the midst of the world. I will show what it means to have

INTRODUCTION

a culture for missions, what it means to live in spiritual separation from the world and yet to reach out to that world, and what it looks like when a church with a covenantal emphasis becomes enflamed with zeal for mission.

I will discuss our covenantal motivation for evangelism and missions in chapter 8. Some might think that a strong conviction concerning the covenant would leave people unmotivated to send many missionaries overseas and zealously reach out to their local communities. But I will argue that the opposite is the case if one has a correct understanding of and takes sweet pleasure in the covenant of grace.

I will conclude the book in chapter 9 by explaining the goal of God with the covenant and missions. Our hope for the full perfection of the covenant in the new heaven and earth serves as further motivation to be busy in sending out missionaries and engaging in local evangelism. When the gospel is preached in all nations, the end will come and we will enjoy the fullness of bliss in God's covenant forever.

STUDY QUESTIONS

1. Can you trace your spiritual lineage back to many consecutive generations of believers?

2. Do you know when and how God began the spiritual line of which you are a part? How did God bring your ancestors into his covenant for the first time?

3. Do you believe God ever establishes his covenant with people who grew up in a pagan or secular context? Why or why not?

4. Is there zeal for world missions in your congregation or denomination? If not, or if it has room to grow, what can you do to help?

BIBLICAL OVERVIEW: ADAM TO NOAH

To begin unfolding the relationship between God's covenant and missions, we need to go back to the very beginning of God's revelation concerning his covenant in the Scriptures.

The Covenant in the Beginning

What do we read in the first few chapters of the Bible? We find the Lord God forming the first man from the dust of the newly created earth, and the first woman from the rib of that man (Gen. 2:7, 21–23). We find God creating the first human beings, a peculiar creature unlike all others, a marvelous unity of body and soul, of rational and moral faculties, an image of God, a mirror of the divine goodness (1:26–28). We behold God fashioning the man and woman this way so that they could walk and talk with their God in a close and warm relationship of fellowship. For God put these fearfully and wonderfully made creatures into the most beautiful place in the cosmos, the garden of Eden, and appeared to them somehow under the canopy of the heavens to walk with them in the cool breeze of the day among the wonders of the earth (2:8; 3:8). We hear him giving

Adam the right to eat the fruit of every tree in the garden, except for the tree of the knowledge of good and evil, for in the day that he would eat of that tree, he would surely die (2:16–17).

I do not intend to write a lengthy discussion of God's covenant with Adam at this point. I will only make a couple of remarks in connection with our subject. First, although you do not find the word "covenant" in these first few chapters of Scripture, it is clear from what the rest of Scripture teaches that God first established his covenant with Adam and Eve in paradise. But contrary to the thinking of many, it was not a covenant of *works*. That is, it was not a pact formed between God and Adam at the time when God commanded Adam concerning those trees. It was not a pact in which God promised to give eternal life to Adam on the condition that Adam perform the work of faithful obedience to God for a certain amount of time. Rather, God established his covenant with Adam and Eve at the moment when he created them. It was a covenant of *creation*, in which God who created them was their God, and they who were made in his image were his people. It was a structured relationship of life and love. The intimate relationship of marriage in which God also created them symbolized their intimate relationship with God.

Second, although the rest of Scripture teaches that God foreordained to condemnation a portion of the human race that would flow from Adam and Eve and foreordained the other portion to eternal life, God nevertheless reveals in the opening chapters of the Bible that his purpose was from the beginning to enter into covenant with *mankind*. God did not in the beginning create a world full of many families or nations and immediately elect one of those nations as his covenantal people while rejecting the rest. But God created one man whom he made the head of the whole human race, then a woman whom he made out of the man, and then he entered into covenant with them.

From that first man and his wife would flow the whole race of mankind, which would unfold itself into many nations, tribes, and tongues. If you are a white-skinned human being like me, next time you see your brown-skinned neighbor, remember that you are both children of Adam and Eve with whom God first established his covenant. Then remember that God has a purpose to establish his covenant with people from every nation, tribe, and tongue of the family of Adam.

The Covenant and the Fall

As we continue to read through Genesis, we soon find that it was not God's purpose to continue his covenant with all the offspring of Adam and Eve in that original state of righteousness. But God's purpose was to reveal the riches of his grace in the Messiah by establishing his covenant with a portion of the children of Adam and Eve who are no better than the other portion but together with them have fallen into sin. Adam fell into sin, by divine appointment, when he ate the forbidden fruit. In Adam, the whole human race fell into sin and became worthy of death. So if you are an American like me, we may never think that we are morally better than our immigrant Mexican or Indian neighbors by nature, but we like them are sinners who deserve the penalty of death. When we witness to them, we must maintain the humble attitude of those who know our own need for salvation and confess that among sinners, "I am chief" (1 Tim. 1:15).

But as Herman Hoeksema put it, Adam and Eve "fell upon Christ who stood behind them," for "the fall of Adam must serve to make room for Christ and for the better covenant."[1] God did not destroy Adam and Eve after they fell into sin, but he sought them when they hid among the trees of the garden, and he issued what Roger Greenway has called "the first missionary call in Scripture" when he called out to Adam: "Where art thou?" (Gen. 3:8–9). Greenway writes: "We see for the first time that God is a *missionary* God in Genesis!"[2]

The children of Adam and Eve have unwittingly followed their example throughout history, vainly trying to cover their nakedness with the fig leaves of the rituals of their heathen religions and hiding from God behind the trees of vain philosophies and carnal attempts to dull the conscience and escape God's judgment. But God calls out to man: "Where art thou?" He sends the preaching of the gospel into the world with that call, putting enmity between the two seeds that would descend from Adam and Eve and establishing his covenant with the seed of the woman.

For when God found Adam and Eve, he confronted them with their sins and then spoke the "mother promise" that he would put enmity between the serpent and the woman, between his seed and her seed, and while the serpent would bruise the heel of the woman's seed, the latter would crush his head (Gen. 3:15). With that promise, God announced his establishment of the covenant of grace with the woman and her seed, for enmity with the devil amounts to friendship with God.

That promise sounds forth particular and universal notes regarding the covenant of grace. On the one hand, God teaches

---

1 Herman Hoeksema, *Reformed Dogmatics*, 2nd ed. (Grandville, MI: Reformed Free Publishing Association, 2004), 1:365, 464.
2 Roger S. Greenway, *Go and Make Disciples! An Introduction to Christian Missions* (Phillipsburg, NJ: P&R Publishing, 1999), 34.

us in that first proclamation of the gospel that he would establish his covenant only with the woman and her seed, not with the devil and his seed. The seed of the woman is ultimately Christ, whose heel Satan would bruise at the cross, but who would crush the head of Satan by his sacrificial death, glorious resurrection, and final coming. The seed of the woman are then those, too, whom God has chosen and redeemed by Christ and called to himself out of the world, both in the Old and New Testament, whom Satan ceases not to persecute, but who are victorious in Christ. Thus, God promises to establish his covenant only with Christ and those who are in Christ.

Homer Hoeksema writes:

> That seed of the woman and that seed of the serpent are from a natural point of view both the woman's seed, for both together make up the human race throughout time. But from now on, that natural seed of the woman will be divided into two camps, into two seeds, from a spiritual point of view. From that spiritual point of view there will be, on the one hand, the spiritual children of the covenant, the holy seed, in the lines of the generations of the elect; that seed in the highest sense is our Lord Jesus Christ.[3]

So, according to his decree of predestination, God here promises to divide all humanity into two spiritual seeds and to establish his covenant with the elect in Christ.

But in this very same place, God also promises to establish his covenant with the whole width and breadth of that

---

3 Homer C. Hoeksema, *Unfolding Covenant History, Vol. 1: From Creation to the Flood*, ed. Mark Hoeksema (Grandville, MI: Reformed Free Publishing Association, 2000), 176.

humanity. After all, it is not only true that the *natural* seed of the woman are all human beings head for head, but it is also true that the *spiritual* seed of the woman include human beings who now live in all four corners of the earth. Adam named his wife Eve "because she was the mother of all living" (Gen. 3:20). Eve, the first woman, was the mother of all human beings. God wants us to see that he has a grand covenantal purpose that must eventually extend to his people throughout the whole of the offspring of Eve in all its vastness and diversity.

Herman Bavinck writes that

> humanity had made a covenant [with the devil] and for its sake broken the covenant with God. God graciously annuls it, puts enmity between the seed of the serpent and the woman's seed, brings the seed of the woman—humanity, that is—back to his side, hence declaring that from Eve will spring a human race and that that race, though it will have to suffer much in the conflict with that evil power, will eventually triumph.[4]

Bavinck was no universalist: he simply recognized the universal note that God sounded in his mother promise. God brings *humanity* back to his side and promises that *humanity* will triumph in the way of conflict with the devil.

God intends to establish his covenant with humanity in Christ. It is particular: with the elect alone. It is also universal: with all families of the human race. God has a grand and glorious vision for his covenant. Do we share his grand vision?

---

4 Herman Bavinck, *Reformed Dogmatics, Vol. 3: Sin and Salvation in Christ*, ed. John Bolt, trans. John Vriend (Grand Rapids, MI: Baker Academic, 2006), 199.

BIBLICAL OVERVIEW: ADAM TO NOAH

The Covenant and the Flood

God shows his vision to us in a striking manner in the history of the flood. The seed of the serpent had in the course of many centuries come to dominate the earth and seemed to vanquish the woman's seed (Gen. 6:1–6). This situation foreshadowed the last days of world history when iniquity will abound everywhere and the wicked will seem to have stamped out the church of Jesus Christ (Matt. 24:12, 36–39). We see this increase of iniquity in our world today, and some of us are of a mind to think that the apparent triumph of evil in formerly Christian lands indicates that the end must be only a few years away, and the mission of the church to the world must be nearly finished. But we know not the day nor the hour of the end.

We certainly live in evil days, like those before the flood. But we may not use that fact to excuse a lack of interest or activity in our mission to preach the gospel to the world. We must remember that also regarding missions we are runners in a race who must press with ever greater force and vigor toward the finish line as we draw closer to it. What the apostle exhorts in Hebrews 12:1–2 applies to missions too: "Let us run with patience the race that is set before us, looking unto Jesus the author and finisher of our faith." What Paul expresses in Philippians 3:14 also applies to missions and ought to be our personal resolve as well: "I press toward the mark for the prize of the high calling of God in Christ Jesus."

But to return to the history of the flood, in those dark days Noah found grace in the eyes of the Lord (Gen. 6:8). God eventually destroyed the wicked world with a flood. But with Noah, his family, and the animals he established his covenant, and he saved them by the waters of the flood in the ark (vv. 17–20). Once again, particular and universal notes are heard in this history. The particularity is seen in the fact that God chose Noah and established his covenant with him but vowed to destroy the wicked in the flood. The universality is seen in the fact that God would continue his covenant through Noah with the whole human race. God saved the human race when he saved the family of Noah and bequeathed a new world to them, born out of the destruction of the old.

The salvation of Noah, his family, and the animals was a type of the salvation of the elect human race in all nations and all living things through the blood of Christ (1 Pet. 3:20–21; Col. 1:20). Christ is the Savior of the world (1 John 4:14). When Christ returns, God will bequeath to those who are in Christ in all nations under heaven the new and everlasting world that will be born out of the fiery destruction of this world.

Herman Hanko wrote regarding the covenant with Noah:

> So often in our altogether proper concern for the salvation of the people of God, we nevertheless fail to see the vast scope of God's work. We become wrapped up in ourselves and are so narrow-minded that we cannot see anything but the salvation of the church. But God's plan of redemption far transcends our boldest conceptions. It is proper that we not lose sight of the fact that we are not the sole objects of God's favor and grace. He takes not only us into the fellowship of his covenant, but he includes in it the whole creation: the birds, the fish, the animals, the lofty firmament studded with stars, the spreading maple, the arching elm, yes, the entire creation about us.[5]

---

5 Herman Hanko, *God's Everlasting Covenant of Grace* (Grand Rapids, MI: Reformed Free Publishing Association, 1988), 64.

BIBLICAL OVERVIEW: ADAM TO NOAH

After the flood, God revealed that he establishes his covenant with the whole cosmos: with Noah and his seed after him and every living creature that came out of the ark with him, the birds, the cattle, and the beasts of the earth (Gen. 9:8–10). God did not mean that he would establish his covenant with *all* the descendants of Noah. He did not establish his relationship of friendship, for example, with wicked Canaan, the grandson of Noah and father of the ungodly Canaanites. He cursed Canaan and later destroyed the Canaanites for their many abominations. But he did establish his bond of sweet fellowship with godly Shem, the firstborn son of Noah, and focused his covenantal purposes on his line throughout the rest of the Old Testament (vv. 25–27). When he revealed his covenant with Noah and his seed, he was pointing forward to Christ, the ultimate Seed of Noah, who would come from the line of Shem.

Nevertheless, when God said after the flood that his covenant is with Noah, his seed after him, and every living creature with him, promising never again to destroy the earth with a flood, he was teaching us the cosmic scope of his covenant. He put the rainbow in the clouds, arching brilliantly from one end of heaven to the other, seeming to embrace the whole globe, as a token of his covenant with the whole cosmos. He would never again destroy the earth with a flood, so that mankind might multiply again and fill the earth and eventually unfold into the many nations he had in mind. His plan was then to extend his covenant to all those nations descended from Noah. So whatever race, nationality, or skin color you are, when you talk to people of another race, nationality, or skin color, remember that the same rainbow arches over us all, and we are all the offspring of Noah with whom God established his covenant after the flood.

In conclusion, the opening chapters of the Bible clearly show both particular and universal aspects of God's covenantal purposes with the world. In Reformed circles, we sometimes focus too narrowly on the former. But when we give more attention to the latter, we may come to a greater appreciation for our worldwide mission mandate as the church and for our personal calling to witness to the world in this present time.

STUDY QUESTIONS

1. God created the human race in covenant with himself. Should that affect the way we think about evangelism with regard to the different races of human beings that exist today? Why?

2. In Genesis 3:15, God promises to put enmity between the seed of the serpent and the seed of the woman and thus to establish his covenant with the latter. Who is included in the "seed of the woman"? Consider the quotations from Homer Hoeksema and Herman Bavinck.

3. How do God's promises to Noah after the flood keep us from being narrowminded in our thinking about his covenant? See Genesis 9:8-17.

BIBLICAL OVERVIEW: ABRAHAM TO CHRIST

When we think of God's covenant with Abraham, it is possible that we overlook the worldwide scope that God reveals in that covenant.

Prior to God's call of the man named Abram, God thwarted the arrogance of men who tried to build a city and tower whose top would reach up to heaven, thereby to make themselves a name and avoid being scattered over the face of the earth. God confused the one language of that day and brought about the birth of new languages, races, ethnicities, and nations. The wonder that God performed at Babel forms the background of his call of Abram.

Abraham and His Seed

God chose and called Abram, a man descended from Noah through the line of Shem, to leave his homeland of Ur of the Chaldees and to go out into a strange country and become the father of the covenantal nation in the Old Testament (Gen. 12:1; Neh. 9:7). God encouraged Abram with the blessed promise to make him a great nation and to bless those who blessed him and curse those who cursed him. God promised to give him and Sarai a son in their old age by a wonder of grace and to multiply their seed like the stars of heaven. God made his covenant with Abram when he passed alone through the two rows of divided animals while Abram slept (Gen. 15:17–18).

We observe in this history the particularity of God's covenant. God *elected* Abram and established his covenant with *him*. God in his decree of election has determined, among the masses of mankind, whom he will draw into his covenant. I stand with those in the Reformed tradition who have taught, on the basis of Scripture and the Reformed creeds, that God establishes his covenant with the elect alone.[1]

God revealed to Abram that he establishes his covenant ultimately with Christ and all who belong to Christ. When I was a child in catechism class, I had to memorize Genesis 17:7, where God says to Abraham: "And I will establish my covenant between me and thee and thy seed after thee in their generations for an everlasting covenant, to be a God unto thee, and to thy seed after thee." In this verse, God promises to establish his covenant not only with Abraham but with his *seed* after him.

When I was a bit older, I learned that this *seed* of Abraham is ultimately *Christ*. That is what the apostle Paul taught in his epistle to the Galatians: "Now to Abraham and his seed were the promises made. He saith not, And to seeds, as of many; but as of one, And to thy seed, which is Christ" (Gal. 3:16). When God promised to establish his covenant with Abraham's seed, he was making that promise to *Christ*. Paul went on in the same chapter to say: "As many of you as have been baptized

---

[1] See, for instance, some of the theologians discussed in David J. Engelsma, *Covenant and Election in the Reformed Tradition* (Jenison, MI: Reformed Free Publishing Association, 2011).

into Christ have put on Christ…and if ye be Christ's, then are ye Abraham's seed, and heirs according to the promise" (vv. 27–29). Thus God promises to establish his covenant with Christ and all who are Christ's, that is, with all the elect.

Having established that truth, go back to Genesis 17:7 and notice that God extends his promise to "thy seed after thee *in their generations.*" God has not elected *all* the children of believers. But God has promised to continue his covenant with the children of believers "in their generations," to establish his covenant from generation to generation in the families of the faithful. The rest of Scripture also testifies of this fundamental truth concerning the way God establishes his covenant. For example: "The mercy of the LORD is from everlasting to everlasting upon them that fear him, and his righteousness unto children's children; to such as keep his covenant, and to those that remember his commandments to do them" (Ps. 103:17–18); "For the promise is unto you, and to your children, and to all that are afar off, even as many as the Lord our God shall call" (Acts 2:39).

A Father of Many Nations

But I believe we have neglected to emphasize another fundamental truth concerning the way God establishes his covenant, a truth revealed in the very same history of Abram. Going back to the first time we read of God calling him, God promised: "In thee shall *all families* of the earth be blessed" (Gen. 12:3). God had just confused the language at Babel and scattered the people. Out of the one original mass of humanity, many new nations and cultures were born, were developing, and were spreading over the earth. Now God comes to Abram with the promise that he will bless *all* those families of the earth in him. Do you hear this universal note in the music of God's covenant? Read on.

God tells Abram: "As for me, behold, my covenant is with thee, and thou shalt be a father of many nations. Neither shall thy name any more be called Abram, but thy name shall be Abraham; for a father of many nations have I made thee" (Gen. 17:4–5). God changed Abram's name to Abraham, which means "father of a multitude" or "father of many," because he promised to make him a father of many nations. God did not merely mean that Abraham would become the biological father of the few nations that sprang from his loins, namely, the Ishmaelites, Israelites, Midianites, Edomites, and others. But God meant that Abraham would become the spiritual father of believing men and women in all nations of the world! God was further unveiling his purpose to establish his covenant throughout the vast diversity of the human race, not just with Israelites, but with people in all nations who have the same faith in Christ that Abraham had. God was further revealing his plan to form a covenant with believers and their seed not just from *one* of the many emerging nations and cultures of the world, but with believers and their seed from *all* of them, who are like the sand on the seashore innumerable!

Paul picks up on this theme in his epistles. Abraham is

11. the father of all them that believe, though they be not circumcised; that righteousness might be imputed unto them also:
12. And the father of circumcision to them who are not of the circumcision only, but who also walk in the steps of that faith of our father Abraham, which he had being yet uncircumcised.

13. For the promise, that he should be the heir of the world, was not to Abraham, or to his seed, through the law, but through the righteousness of faith. (Rom. 4:11–13)

Paul calls Abraham the father of all believers, whether circumcised Jews or uncircumcised Gentiles, because Abraham believed in the Lord *before* he was circumcised.

Paul does not call Abraham the father of all believers because he was the first believer in the world. Abel believed long before Abraham. But he calls Abraham the father of all believers because he was the man to whom and through whom God was pleased to reveal for the first time in history, even prior to the birth of the Jewish nation, that all who believe in him as Abraham did will be justified and saved into his everlasting covenant. "And he [Abraham] believed in the Lord; and he [the Lord] counted it to him for righteousness" (Gen. 15:6). God had promised to bring forth a Seed from Abraham's own bowels, Christ, the heir of the whole world, and in that Seed, Abraham and all who walk in the same steps of faith that he did would be counted righteous and heirs of the world.

God would have us see in his promise to Abraham a revelation of his purpose to justify the heathen by faith and gather them into his covenant of grace. "And the scripture, foreseeing that God would justify the heathen through faith, preached before the gospel unto Abraham, saying, In thee shall all nations be blessed. So then they which be of faith are blessed with faithful Abraham" (Gal. 3:8–9).

Have we paused long enough to contemplate the meaning of all this in connection with our covenantal theology? Have we done justice in our thinking about the covenant to this promise of God to make Abraham a father of many nations? The promise of God to establish his covenant with Abraham and his seed after him in their generations is the foundation of our calling to baptize our infants and train our children in the ways of God in the home and school.

But the promise of God to make Abraham a father of many nations, to extend his covenant from Abraham outward into all the nations of the earth, is the foundation of our calling to evangelize the lost and send missionaries to the ends of the earth with the gospel of Christ. It must live in our minds and hearts that God purposes to establish his covenant not only with us and our children after us in our generations, but also with his elect who are still lost in the nations around us, both afar off and nearby. We must have an equal amount of zeal for the raising of our children in the ways of the Lord and the evangelization of the world around us.

In the spring of 2023, I had the privilege of being one of the speakers at a missions conference in Hudsonville, Michigan. The other speaker was Jonathan Mahtani, one of my colleagues in the ministry. In the published version of his speech, he writes: "This evangelistic character of the covenant is found everywhere in Scripture, indeed even in the Old Testament. Although it is true that the covenant revealed to the Old Testament people emphasized an inward-looking view, there was already then an evangelistic character." He reminds us that "we do injustice to the character of the covenant" when we quote Genesis 17:7, where God promises to continue his covenant with Abraham's seed after him in their generations, and ignore verses 4–5, where God promises to make Abraham a father of many nations. "Abraham and the Jewish people with him cherished the promises of God to gather His people from their generations, but they also eagerly anticipated the evangelistic character of that covenant soon to be displayed in the gathering of the Gentiles."[2] After hearing that speech, I remember thinking to myself that he had just delivered the heart of the content of this book.

The Nations to Flow into Mount Zion

In the rest of the Old Testament after Abraham, God focused his covenantal purposes on the descendants of Abraham through Isaac and Jacob: the nation of Israel. He redeemed them from the land of Egypt, the house of bondage, brought them through the wilderness into the land of promise, and separated them from all the other nations as his precious covenantal people. He told them that he had chosen them to be a special people to himself above all the other peoples on the face of the earth merely because he had loved them (Deut. 7:6–8). God's election of Israel as his covenantal people in the Old Testament is one of the most striking proofs of election and reprobation in the Scriptures. God chose Israel and rejected the other nations. God teaches us clearly that he is not interested in establishing his covenant with all men head for head, but only with the elect whom he loves.

The Dutch Reformed missiologist J. H. Bavinck wrote that

> at first sight the Old Testament appears to offer little basis for the idea of missions. This part of the Bible speaks of bloody wars and the annihilation of various peoples; it

---

2 Jonathan Mahtani, "The Evangelistic Character of the Covenant," *Standard Bearer* 99, no. 19 (August 2023): 451–452.

appears to have very little room for mercy, nor does it seem ready to grant the blessings of the gospel to the heathen… Yet, if we investigate the Old Testament more thoroughly, it becomes clear that the future of the nations is a point of the greatest concern…This indeed cannot be otherwise, for from the first page to the last the Bible has the whole world in view, and its divine plan of salvation is unfolded as pertaining to the whole world.[3]

Indeed, throughout the Old Testament, God preserved in the hearts of his people the promise to Abraham, the hope of the extension of his covenant into all the world. He inspired them to express their hope in soul-stirring psalms, singing with hopeful joy: "All the ends of the world shall remember and turn unto the LORD: and all the kindreds of the nations shall worship before thee" (Ps. 22:27); "Let the people praise thee, O God; let all the people praise thee. O let the nations be glad and sing for joy" (67:3–4). And concerning the Messiah: "He shall have dominion also from sea to sea, and from the river unto the ends of the earth. They that dwell in the wilderness shall bow before him; and his enemies shall lick the dust…Yea, all kings shall fall down before him: all nations shall serve him" (72:8–11); "Say among the heathen that the LORD reigneth" (96:10).

God also inspired the prophets to foretell the day when God would open his covenant to the nations to gather them in. The prophets lived in days when the nations were wicked and mighty, physical and spiritual threats to God's covenantal people. But they prophesied the coming of a day when those nations would flow into Mount Zion, being subdued by the

---

3   J. H. Bavinck, *An Introduction to the Science of Missions*, trans. David Hugh Freeman (Nutley, NJ: Presbyterian and Reformed Publishing, 1977), 11.

word of God, beating their swords into plowshares and their spears into pruninghooks, and being at peace with one another in the church (Isa. 2:2-4; Mic. 4:1-4). In that day, there would be a highway out of Egypt to Assyria, and the Assyrian would come to Egypt, and the Egyptians would serve with the Assyrians, and Israel would be the third with Egypt and Assyria. The Lord would bless them, saying: "Blessed be Egypt my people, and Assyria the work of my hands, and Israel mine inheritance" (Isa. 19:23-25).

God promised to send the Messiah not merely as the head of the covenant for the Jews but "for a covenant of the people, for a light of the Gentiles; to open the blind eyes, to bring out the prisoners from the prison, and them that sit in darkness out of the prison house" (Isa. 42:6-7). The last prophets of the Old Testament, too, foretold the great day of the inflow of the nations into God's covenant: "Yea, many people and strong nations shall come to seek the LORD of hosts in Jerusalem, and to pray before the LORD" (Zech. 8:22).

A Savior for All Nations, Tribes, and Tongues

Finally, at the high point of world history, God fulfilled his promise by sending his own Son into human flesh in the womb of a virgin daughter of Abraham: "For verily he took not on him the nature of angels; but he took on him the seed of Abraham" (Heb. 2:16). God made plain at the time of the birth of Christ that this was a Savior for the world and not just for Israel. The angel sang to the shepherds outside Bethlehem: "Behold, I bring you good tidings of great joy, which shall be to all people. For unto you is born this day in the city of David, a Savior, which is Christ the Lord" (Luke 2:10-11). The good tidings of salvation that brings sinners into the covenant "shall be to all people" because God wills to establish his covenant among all the peoples of the earth.

A star appeared in the East to herald the birth of the Savior to Gentile wise men, who were likely Babylonian or Persian scholars of the heavens. The star prompted them to seek the babe who was born to be King of the Jews, that is, of the *spiritual* children of Abraham, which included them. When aged Simeon held the Christ child in his arms, he spoke by the Spirit: "Lord, now lettest thou thy servant depart in peace, according to thy word: For mine eyes have seen thy salvation, which thou hast prepared before the face of all people; a light to lighten the Gentiles, and the glory of thy people Israel" (Luke 2:29–32). God sounds the universal note in the music of his covenant in these texts, which ought to drive us out into the world to proclaim the gospel message to all peoples.

Jesus himself taught us in many places that God wills to establish his covenant with people in all nations. It is true that his first commission to the disciples forbade them to go into the way of the Gentiles and restricted their preaching to the "lost sheep of the house of Israel" (Matt. 10:5–6). But we may not so apply this command of Jesus as to excuse our lack of missions or disinterest in missions to the heathen by claiming that Christ only sends us to preach the truth to lost sheep in other churches who are being fed lies.

There is certainly a need for church reformation work. For example, there is a need to call lost sheep who have swallowed false gospels to spit them out and to graze safely in the green pastures of the pure gospel of Christ. But there is also a need and calling to go into the way of the Gentiles, to seek the lost sheep among the Gentiles, for Christ gave a greater commission just before he ascended into heaven, and that leaves no uncertainty about where we must go with the gospel. Also, Jesus calls us "the light of the world" who must let our light shine before men (Matt. 5:13-16).

Jesus once marveled at the faith that a Gentile centurion had, and he proclaimed: "Verily I say unto you, I have not found so great faith, no, not in Israel. And I say unto you, that many shall come from the east and west, and shall sit down with Abraham, and Isaac, and Jacob, in the kingdom of heaven. But the children of the kingdom shall be cast out into outer darkness" (Matt. 8:10-12). Jesus teaches that God has a purpose to draw people into his covenantal kingdom from the vast nations of India, China, and others in the East and those of Europe and America in the West.

Jesus died on the cross as the head and mediator of the covenant of grace and the Savior of the world all at once. He died not only for Jews but also for Gentiles. He shed his blood, the blood of the new covenant, for the remission of sins for *many* (Matt. 26:28; Mark 14:24; Luke 22:20), not only us and our children, but also the millions of the heathen world whom God elected to salvation. He is the Lamb of God who takes away the sin of the *world* (John 1:29), not just of one denomination, or one ethnic group, or one nation. God so loved the world that he gave his only begotten Son, that *whosoever* believes in him, through the preaching of the gospel that goes forth within and outside the sphere of the covenant, shall not perish but have everlasting life (John 3:16).

God will have *all* kinds of men to be saved and to come to the knowledge of the truth, not just Dutch or Americans or Canadians, but also Filipinos and Burmese and Singaporeans and Africans (1 Tim. 2:4). Therefore, God provided one mediator between himself and mankind, the man Christ Jesus, who gave himself a ransom for *all* (vv. 5–6). Jesus did not die for every human being without exception, but only for the elect. But God willed that the millions or billions of the elect for whom he died would come from all families of the earth.

The Canons of Dordt teach that it was the purpose of God that the saving power of the death of Christ would extend to those only "who were from eternity chosen to salvation, and given to Him by the Father." But the same article states that the blood of the cross, by which he confirmed the new covenant, would redeem those elect "out of every people, tribe, nation, and language."[4] Thus the purpose of God was to lay the foundation of his covenant in the blood of Christ, the chief cornerstone who gave his life a ransom for all the elect throughout all time and space, so that he might bring each of them as living stones into the fellowship of that covenant through faith by his word and Spirit. Therefore, the task of missions is to go into all the nations and preach the gospel of Christ crucified, for thereby God establishes his covenant with the world of his elect and bestows his covenantal blessings on each one.

Go into All the World

After Jesus rose again from the dead and received all authority in heaven and on earth, he issued his last and great commission to his eleven disciples: go into all the world, preach my gospel to everyone, call everyone to repent and believe, and make disciples in all nations, baptizing in the name of the Father, of the Son, and of the Holy Ghost, teaching them to observe all things

---

4 Canons of Dordt 2.8, in Schaff, *Creeds of Christendom*, 3:587.

that I have taught you. And lo, I am with you always, even unto the end of the world. Amen (see Matt. 28:18–20; Mark 16:15–16; Luke 24:47–48).

Jesus showed that the mission of God to establish his covenant in all nations would come to pass through the witness of the church. God would go before the apostles and evangelists in the person of his Holy Spirit to regenerate the hearts of those whom he would save. He would then call them through the gospel that he sends us to preach and bring them by a living faith into the fellowship of his covenant. Baptism must be administered to heathen converts and their households as a sign and seal of the covenant into which God has brought them.

When Jesus poured out the Holy Spirit on Pentecost to inaugurate this last epoch of world history, Peter stood up and proclaimed to Jews from every nation under heaven: "The promise is unto you, and to your children, *and to all that are afar off, even as many as the Lord our God shall call*" (Acts 2:38–39). On the one hand, the promise is limited to those whom the Lord our God shall call to a living faith in Christ through the Holy Spirit working in their hearts, to the elect, for "whom he did predestinate, them he also called: and whom he called, them he also justified: and whom he justified, them he also glorified" (Rom. 8:30). But on the other hand, Peter preached at the dawn of the New Testament that the promise is not limited to us and our children in our generations but extends outward to all the elect who are afar off in heathen nations.

God will realize his promise to make Abraham a father of many nations through the mission work of the church in this last era of history. We live in the age of covenantal expansion to the ends of the earth. What an exciting time to live! What a great task has been given us!

STUDY QUESTIONS

1. In Genesis 17:7, God promises to establish his covenant with Abraham and his seed after him in their generations. Who is included in the "seed of Abraham"? See Galatians 3:26-29.

2. In Genesis 17:4-5, God promises to make Abraham "a father of many nations." Why did God call him that? What does this have to do with missions today?

3. Read the psalms and prophecies quoted in this chapter. What do they reveal about the hope of Old Testament Israel? How do they apply to us today?

4. How does biblical teaching concerning the death of Christ reveal God's plan to establish his covenant with people of all nations? Read the verses about Christ's death mentioned in this chapter and Canons of Dordt, head 2, article 8.

5. Is the great commission a mandate of the covenant? Why or why not?

3

GOD'S ETERNAL COUNSEL, COVENANT, AND MISSIONS

We ended the last chapter by noting that God sent Christ to accomplish salvation for *all* families of the earth in fulfillment of his promise to Abraham, and Christ commissioned us to go into all the world to preach the good news of what he has accomplished. We now turn again to the teaching of our Lord and zero in on his statement that as God sent him into the world, so he also sends us into the world. The English word "mission" comes from a Latin word that means "sending." Therefore, we may put it this way: as Jesus went into the world on a mission from God, so we must go into the world on a mission from Jesus. As he was sent on his mission by the eternal will and counsel of God, so we are sent on ours by the will of our Lord Jesus Christ.

As My Father Sent Me into the World…

In the texts announcing that God sent his Son into the world, Reformed theologians have seen a revelation of the eternal covenant within the Trinity, which they called in Latin the *pactum salutis* (i.e., the "covenant of redemption"). For example,

Jesus said in his high priestly prayer: "As thou hast *sent* me into the world, even so have I also *sent* them into the world" (John 17:18). He appeared to his disciples after his resurrection and said: "Peace be unto you: as my Father hath *sent* me, even so *send* I you" (John. 20:21). The apostle Paul wrote: "And when the fulness of the time was come, God *sent* forth His Son…to redeem them that were under the law" (Gal. 4:4–5). The apostle John wrote: "And we have seen and do testify that the Father *sent* the Son to be the Saviour of the world" (1 John 4:14).

The theologians who teach the *pactum salutis* say these texts reveal an eternal covenant within the Trinity between the Father and the Son.[1] They certainly do not all define this covenant in exactly the same way or with exactly the same terms. But they generally agree that it is an eternal pact or agreement between the Father and the Son (and some try to include the Holy Spirit). In this pact, the Father eternally assigns to the Son the work of reconciling a fallen world to himself, and the Son eternally accepts his assignment.

Like the covenant with us, this covenant of redemption, too, is considered to be a *pact* or *contract* with parties, promises, and conditions. The Father and Son are the contracting parties. The Father promises to glorify the Son on the condition that the Son will go into the world, become a man through the incarnation, and accomplish the salvation of the elect through his death. The Son accepts the mission assigned to him by the Father and promises to obey his will and give his life a ransom

---

[1] See Hoeksema, *Reformed Dogmatics*, 1:403-453. He describes the *pactum salutis* as taught by certain theologians (Petrus van Mastricht, Francis Turretin, Wilhelmus à Brakel, Charles Hodge, Geerhardus Vos, Herman Bavinck, Louis Berkhof, and Abraham Kuyper) and evaluates the doctrine both positively and negatively.

for many on the condition that the Father will keep his end of the bargain. This, we are told, is the meaning of the Father *sending* his Son into the world.

According to this view, by coming into the world in the incarnation and accomplishing salvation by his death on the cross, the Son has fulfilled his end of the agreement, and by raising him from the dead and exalting him to his right hand, the Father has fulfilled his end of the agreement. Thus, the eternal covenant between the Father and Son has been fulfilled and has essentially fallen away, because it was a means to an end, and the end has been accomplished. Now, when Jesus says that in like manner he sends us into the world to preach the gospel in all nations, some theologians see God employing missions to establish a similar kind of covenant with men on the basis of the fulfilled covenant between the Father and Son.[2] Like the covenant between the Father and Son, they view this covenant, too, as a pact or contract with parties, promises, and conditions.

Through missionary preaching, God announces the promise of his covenant, his end of the bargain, which he makes to all who hear the message: I promise to glorify you with eternal life on one condition, that you believe in Jesus Christ as your Lord and Savior. Whoever responds to that promise by believing in Christ and persevering to the end of his life has fulfilled the other end of the bargain, and when he enters heaven, the covenant with him falls away.

---

[2] See Davi Charles Gomes, "The Source of Mission in the Covenant of Redemption," in *A Covenantal Vision for Global Mission*, 3–19. In this essay, Brazilian Reformed theologian Davi Gomes calls the *pactum salutis* the source of the mission of the church, which is "to sound clearly the glorious music of the gospel to the ears of the listening world" (16). He refers to theologians such as C. Hodge, G. Vos, and Richard Muller to support his conviction of the traditional view of the *pactum salutis*.

As I acknowledged earlier, the theologians who hold to the *pactum salutis* do not all define it the same way and would not all subscribe to the version I have outlined here. But there is widespread agreement that the nature of both the covenant within the Trinity and the covenant between God and man is a pact with parties, promises, and conditions. It is a means to an end, and once that end is accomplished, the covenant as such falls away.

The error of the *pactum salutis* is in its definition of the covenant and thus in its confusion of the eternal *decree* of the triune God with the eternal *covenant* of the triune God. Wrongly defining God's covenant as a pact with parties, promises, and conditions has led many theologians to make a serious mistake in their exegesis of the texts that say Jesus did the will of him who sent him. For example: "I seek not mine own will, but the will of the Father which hath sent me" (John 5:30); "I came down from heaven, not to do mine own will, but the will of him that sent me" (6:38). Some have interpreted these words of Jesus to mean that the second person of the Trinity came not to do his own will, but the will of the First Person, because it was the will of the Father that the Son go into the world. Saying that the eternal Son had to *obey* the will of his eternal Father leads in the direction of a sort of subordinationism, at least implicitly, as it seems to put the Son under the Father.

The truth is that the Father, Son, and Spirit all share the whole divine essence, and they will the whole of the divine will. None is greater than the other, and none must obey the will of the other. What then did Jesus mean? He meant: "I came down from heaven and into human nature not to do mine own *human* will but the will of *God* who sent me."

GOD'S ETERNAL COUNSEL, COVENANT, AND MISSIONS

God's Will to Reveal His Covenant by Establishing a Covenant with Us through Christ

The doctrine of the *pactum salutis*, however, does point us in the direction of an important truth that must be understood and heartily confessed. There *is* an eternal covenant within the Trinity between the Father and the Son through the Holy Spirit. God *has* eternally decreed to send his Son into the world to reveal that covenant by establishing a covenant with men and women in all nations. But to understand the essence of God's own covenant within the Trinity, one must understand the essence of God's covenant with us.

God has revealed that his covenant with us is not a pact or contract, but a relationship of structured fellowship in which God is our God and we are his people; God is our Father and we are his children.[3] God reveals the essence of the covenant in Scripture by the oft-repeated promise "I will be your God, and you will be my people," or "I will be a Father unto you, and you will be my sons and daughters" (for example, see Gen. 17:7; Ex. 29:45; Jer. 31:33; 2 Cor. 6:18; Rev. 21:3). If the covenant that God establishes with us is a relation of love like that between a father and his children, we cannot help but infer from the names of the persons of the Trinity, especially *Father* and *Son*, that the covenant within the Godhead, too, must be such a relation of love.

---

3   One thing in the essay of Davi Gomes that caught my eye as a Protestant Reformed pastor was his positive reference to the teaching of Herman Hoeksema that the covenant in its essence is "the most intimate communion of friendship in which God reflects his own covenant life in his relation to the creature" (10). In the end, I was disappointed to discover that Gomes still regards the covenant as a pact with parties, promises, and conditions. He believes communion with God is the *goal* of the covenant rather than the *essence* of the covenant.

The relationship between a father and his children cannot be defined as a pact or contract with parties, promises, and conditions. Rather, it is a personal relationship of love in which a father who begets children with his wife dwells with them in intimate fellowship in their home. Our relationship as Christian parents with our children is but a dim reflection of the real covenant within the Trinity, the eternal bond of fellowship between the Father and the Son through the Holy Spirit.

Now, before we attempt to penetrate deeper into this truth, let us pause to acknowledge that we stand on holy ground here and must proceed with care. Who are we, after all, to presume to understand such sublime mysteries of the transcendent God, concerning the intra-trinitarian life of him who made the whole world and holds it in his hand? We are little specks of dust on earth in the midst of the vast universe that he spoke into existence. As we draw near to the being of God, I hear him warning, as it were out of the midst of the burning bush, that we draw not any closer than he is pleased to allow. Take off your shoes, he says to us, for this place where you stand is holy ground. At the same time, I hear the encouraging word of our Lord Jesus that this is life eternal, to *know* the only true God and Jesus Christ whom he has sent. May God thus forbid that we step over the boundaries of his revelation and begin to speculate about secrets he does not tell us in the Bible. May God help us to reason within the limits of what he has taught about himself in Holy Scripture.

If God has made clear, as I believe he has, that his own covenant is not a *pact* among the persons of the Trinity providing for the salvation of the world, then how do we explain the texts that speak of God sending his Son to be the Savior of the world?

We understand them to refer to the gracious will of the *whole* Trinity to send the Son as the Savior of sinners, that he would die to save the elect from our sins and give us the right to live with God in his covenant, that he would bring us through his Spirit into living union with himself, and thereby into everlasting communion with the triune God in his covenant.

The problem with the *pactum salutis* is that it confuses the covenant of the triune God with the decree of the triune God to send the Son.[4] The covenant within the Trinity is the relation of fellowship in which all three persons eternally dwell with each other. The will of God to send the Son into the world is something else. It is that glorious decree of all three persons of the Godhead that the Son will be the one to go into the world as the Savior and Mediator of the covenant.

Can we wrap our minds around all of this? We believe that God is three persons in one essence, and these three persons are coequal, coeternal, and coessential. We believe that the persons in the Godhead are intimately bound to each other in love in an eternal covenant as Father, Son, and Holy Spirit. We believe that God eternally decreed all things that come to pass in time, including the establishment of his covenant with the elect in Christ and the gathering of the elect out of the whole world through missions.

---

4   In his essay, Gomes writes: "Herman Hoeksema adds further color to this image [of the *pactum salutis*, which Hoeksema calls the 'decree of the covenant']." Gomes quotes from *Reformed Dogmatics* where Hoeksema calls this decree that which "dominates all other decrees of God concerning the ultimate end of all things as God has conceived it in His counsel. Instead of a decree concerning the means…[it] is the decree concerning the end of all things" (11). However, Gomes follows other theologians in confusing the actual covenant within the Trinity with God's decree to share that covenant with others outside himself.

In light of all that, what does Jesus, the incarnate Son, reveal about God when he says that God sent him into the world? This: that God the Father, God the Son, and God the Holy Spirit, who share the whole divine nature and will, eternally decreed to share their own covenant with a portion of fallen humanity and to send the Son to open the way for us into that covenant by his death on the cross. God the Father, God the Son, and God the Holy Spirit eternally willed this *as one*, as they will all things that come to pass. The Father, who eternally begets the Son, wills to send the Son into the world in order to redeem his elect and bring us into God's covenant. The Son, who eternally rests in the bosom of his Father, wills to go into the world to give his life as a ransom for us and confirm the covenant in his blood. The Holy Spirit, who eternally proceeds from the Father and the Son, wills to bring about the conception of the Son in human nature in the womb of the virgin Mary and to go into the hearts of the elect to bring them into the living experience of life in God's covenant.

What a profound wonder! Before the foundation of the world, all three persons of the Trinity dwelled together in a covenant of life and love and willed with one accord to create a world and to share with others, in the way of sin and grace, the cross and the crown, the blessed life that they enjoy. If it were possible to listen to the conversations of the Father, Son, and Spirit in their blessed covenantal life together, what would we hear? We can only imagine what it sounds like when these three holies of infinite perfection converse with one another with one mind about their glorious decrees and plans for the universe and the covenant. How good and pleasant it is when they, dwelling together in unity, dialogue with each other about these things that matter so much to them without a hint of discord or argument!

GOD'S ETERNAL COUNSEL, COVENANT, AND MISSIONS

We cannot fathom the bottomless depth and boundless height of bliss that the three persons enjoy in their perfect relationship with each other. We experience only a small taste of that when we as fathers talk with our children about the most important things in life and make plans together with one mind and in a spirit of love. That is only a dim reflection because we are not always of one mind and do not always show love for each other. With God it is otherwise. The three persons of the Trinity dwell together in sweet covenantal fellowship and have determined with one will that the Son will go into the world by the power of the Holy Spirit to make a way for people of all kinds to dwell with God forever.

...Even So Do I Send You into the World

Now, to connect this to our mission as the church in the world, Jesus said that *as* the Father sent him into the world, *even so* does he send us into the world. Jesus is the chief missionary. His mission accomplished has become the basis of our mission mandate. As he (the Christ) obeyed the will of God, went into the world, and accomplished the salvation that will usher the nations into the covenant, even so we (as Christians) must obey the will of Jesus, go into the world, and announce that salvation whereby the nations are drawn into the covenant.

Jesus teaches us to see his mission to the world as the example that we must follow. His mission involved self-sacrifice, self-denial, and suffering. He did not remain in his heavenly comfort zone, but he humbled himself and took on the form of a servant. Indeed, he gave up his life in order that God may justly draw sinners in all nations into his covenant. Are we willing and ready to sacrifice ourselves, to deny ourselves, and to suffer for his sake? Are we ready and willing to count the cost and move out of our earthly comfort zones as his servants? Whoever will save his life will lose it, but whoever will lose his life for Jesus' sake will find it (Matt. 16:25). *As* he was sent into the world, *even so* he sends us into the world.

Jesus also means to teach us that his accomplishment of *his* mission ought to motivate us to carry out *ours*. He who was rich became poor for us so that through his poverty we might be rich (2 Cor. 8:9)! He came into the world for us and gave his life for us so that through his suffering we might enter the everlasting covenant and live with God forever! We do not need to perform any works whatsoever to make ourselves worthy of life and acceptable to God. Jesus has done it all. Therefore, the yoke that Jesus places on us is easy and the burden is light. He does not call us to accomplish salvation, which is impossible for us, but only to go forth and proclaim everywhere that it is finished. *As* he was sent into the world, *even so* are we sent into the world.

The ministers of the gospel are sent to preach the gospel of Christ and call sinners to repentance and faith, both nearby in established congregations and afar off on foreign mission fields, as the Lord directs our way. However, let us not forget that all believers and followers of Jesus, whatever our vocation might be, are also in our day-to-day lives sent to sound forth the gospel that we hear in church to the neighbor next door, the coworker in the next cubicle, or the unbeliever sitting next to us in the truck, as we have opportunity.

The grand covenantal purpose of God is not only for us and our children in our generations. It embraces the whole world and reaches unto the ends of the earth. "For God sent not his Son into the world to condemn the world; but that the world through him might be saved" (John 3:17). Therefore, the

GOD'S ETERNAL COUNSEL, COVENANT, AND MISSIONS

Son sends us into the world, too, to teach all nations and baptize those who believe in the name of the Father, and the Son, and the Holy Ghost.[5]

STUDY QUESTIONS

1. After reading and pondering this chapter, what do you believe Jesus meant when he said "my Father sent me into the world"? Does this reveal an eternal pact between the Father and Son for the salvation of the world? Why or why not? See John 3:16-17, John 17:18, Galatians 4:4-5, and 1 John 4:14.

2. Is it biblical to say there is a covenant that binds the Father, Son, and Holy Spirit to each other within the Trinity? Do the names "Father," "Son," and "Spirit" give us a clue about the nature of such a covenant?

3. What are some similarities and differences between the mission God sent Jesus to accomplish in this world and the mission Jesus sends us to accomplish in the world? How are these missions connected to his plan to establish a covenant with men?

---

5 The main point of the essay of Davi Gomes, which has also been the main point of this chapter, is that the glorious mission of God, his eternal purpose to send his Son to save the world of those whom he gave him out of every nation, tribe, and tongue, is the source of our mission to proclaim the gospel of that salvation in all the world. He asks the rhetorical question: "Does this instrument of God's glorious grace [the church] make music only for its own sake? If its mission is rooted in the very movement of the Trinity outside himself, it is only natural that it must also be a movement that expresses the beautiful music of grace to all of creation" (15).

4

GOD'S TWO WAYS OF ESTABLISHING HIS COVENANT

In 2019, when I was living with my family on a mission field in the Philippines, the Lord gave us our fifth child, a baby girl. I remember being struck at that time by the two ways God was pleased to use us for the establishment of his covenant. On the one hand, my wife and I both grew up in a line of generations that God began drawing a long time ago somewhere back in the Netherlands, traced across the Atlantic Ocean through Dutch immigration, and brought all the way down to us. As we held our baby girl in our hands, we believed the truth that God establishes his covenant with believers and their seed after them in their generations, and we brought her to receive the sign of the covenant, holy baptism.

But at the very same time, I was serving as a missionary in the Philippines in the midst of many who were born and raised in the sphere of false religion but who came to a true faith in Christ through the preaching of the gospel. As we lived among these first- or second-generation believers and their children, I was struck by this other truth, that in these last days, God also establishes his covenant with lost sinners out in the world through missions.

Two Truths

On the occasion of baptizing our daughter in the Filipino church where we were stationed in Metro Manila, being struck by these two truths, I decided to preach on Acts 2:39, "The promise is unto you, and to your children, and to all that are afar off, even as many as the Lord our God shall call." In Reformed circles, we appeal to this text as proof that in the New Testament God still promises to establish his covenant with adult believers *and* their children, *while* they are still children, so we ought to baptize the infants of believers. We have been trained well by our Reformed confessions, which cite this text in support of the doctrine of infant baptism.[1] If the promise is not only to adult believers but also to our children, then they as well as we are included in the covenant and ought to be baptized.

But there is another truth taught in Acts 2:39, and that also motivated me to preach it that Sunday of our daughter's baptism and again on many more Sundays in various churches in the U.S. when we visited them while on furlough. The promise of salvation into the everlasting covenant, according to this verse, is also to all who are afar off, even as many as the Lord our God shall call. The Lord had sent me to the Philippines to preach the gospel and call sinners to repent and believe in Christ, just as he has sent multitudes of other missionaries into many lands for the last twenty centuries and will continue to do until he comes again. Why? Because the promise is also for all whom the Lord will call but who are yet "strangers from the

---

1 For example, see Heidelberg Catechism Q&A 74, in *Confessions and Church Order*, 111; Form for the Administration of Baptism, in *Confessions and Church Order*, 259; and the Westminster Confession of Faith Chapter 28, in Schaff, *Creeds of Christendom*, 3:662-663.

GOD'S TWO WAYS OF ESTABLISHING HIS COVENANT

covenants of promise, having no hope, and without God in the world" (Eph. 2:12).

There are two ways in which God establishes his covenant in the New Testament, and we must not neglect to understand and emphasize both, because they both involve weighty callings for the church. As Wilbur Bruinsma writes:

> Reformed churches must be fully aware that there are two distinct, yet interrelated, ways that the Son of God gathers His church in the new dispensation of the covenant. The one means is the faithful nurturing of the children of the church by believing parents and by the church itself...But the church may never ignore the other command of God's covenant: "Go ye into all the world, and preach the gospel to every creature" (Mark 16:15). Equally important to the gathering in of the church in the new dispensation is diligent labor in the whole area of missions.[2]

In a recently published book, Bruinsma devotes a chapter to the doctrine of these two distinct yet interrelated ways that the Son of God gathers his church in the New Testament. He explains that "in the Old Testament, God had established his covenant with his people from one generation to the next only *within the nation of Israel*." God revealed through Peter in Acts 2:39 that he would continue to establish his covenant with Jewish believers in their generations in the New Testament. But God also revealed through Peter that from now on the promise of his covenant would also be with those who are afar off, as many as he will call:

---

2   Wilbur Bruinsma, "Defining Missions," *Standard Bearer* 84, no. 4 (November 15, 2007): 91.

Instead of establishing his covenant with one people and one nation of the earth, now God enters into fellowship with his chosen people from all nations. Unless we are so focused on our own little corner of the world with little interest in our confession, "I believe a holy catholic (universal) church," we are able to see that this has become a reality today.[3]

It is the burden of this book to raise awareness of this truth in our minds as Reformed people.

The Covenant with Believers and Their Seed in Israel

In the old dispensation, God operated in a narrower manner. God gathered his people almost exclusively from the nation of Israel for many centuries before Christ came, and he gathered them almost exclusively in one way, through the instruction of the children of believers. God had chosen Abraham, Isaac, and Jacob and, organically speaking, the nation of Israel. God had established his covenant with them and promised to do so with their seed after them in their generations (Gen. 17:7).

God had expressed as a vitally important demand of his covenant that parents must diligently teach their children all the oracles that he revealed to Moses, talking about them while sitting in their houses, while walking by the way, when lying down, and when rising up (Deut. 6:7). God continued his covenant with Israelite believers and their seed in their generations, but he visited the iniquity of fathers upon their children and

---

[3] Wilbur Bruinsma, *Life in the Covenant in Family, Church, and World* (Jenison, MI: Reformed Free Publishing Association, 2023), 119–120.

GOD'S TWO WAYS OF ESTABLISHING HIS COVENANT

cut off the generations of the unfaithful who impenitently worshipped the idols of the heathen and taught their children to do likewise. At times, God raised up faithful men to lead a reformation in Israel and restore the pure teaching of the Scriptures and the right worship of Jehovah. Nevertheless, God did not yet raise up or send out from Israel an army of missionaries to extend his covenant into all the world.

On a few occasions, though, he did give Israel glimpses and reminders of his ultimate purpose to do so. When he was about to destroy the Canaanites for their great abominations and give the promised land to Israel, he called Rahab the harlot from the wall of Jericho and grafted her into his covenant. "And Joshua saved Rahab the harlot alive, and her father's household, and all that she had; and she dwelleth in Israel even unto this day" (Josh. 6:25). In the evil days of the judges, he providentially ruled over the sojourn of Elimelech and Naomi in a heathen land during a famine in order to graft Ruth the Moabitess into his covenant and bring her to Boaz as his wife. "So Boaz took Ruth, and she was his wife: and when he went in unto her, the Lord gave her conception, and she bare a son" and became a mother in Israel (Ruth 4:13). In the time of King Jeroboam II of Israel, God did an extraordinary thing for the Old Testament and sent Jonah to call heathen Nineveh to repentance. "Arise, go to Nineveh, that great city, and cry against it; for their wickedness is come up before me" (Jonah 1:2). Jonah did not want God to graft the Ninevites into his covenant, so he fled toward Tarshish, and the rest of the story we know.

But these were all exceptions in the old covenant. God was giving reminders and glimpses of what he planned to do in the great day of the Lord. But throughout the long ages of the old dispensation, God established his covenant almost exclusively within Israel with believers and their seed in their generations.

The Enlargement of the Covenant in All the World

That changed when the Messiah came into the world, and this we must allow to sink deeply into our minds and hearts. When Christ came, God made abundantly clear that this was the dawn of the last era of history in which he would enlarge his covenant by establishing it with men and women in all nations of the world through missions. Jesus himself said: "Many shall come from the east and west, and shall sit down with Abraham, and Isaac, and Jacob, in the kingdom of heaven" (Matt. 8:11), that is, many from all nations will flow into the covenant. God nowhere revealed that he was ending the way of gathering his people that he used in the old covenant: the instruction of the children of believers in the home and synagogue. But God did reveal that he was inaugurating a new way of gathering his people that he used hardly at all in the old covenant: the sending of missionaries into all the world to preach the gospel to all.

Since the dawn of the new dispensation, God has been establishing his covenant in two ways and, if you will, in two directions. First, God continued to establish his covenant with believers and their seed in their generations. There was continuity in this regard when God caused the old covenant to fade away and the new covenant to rise up through the death, resurrection, and ascension of Christ and his outpouring of the Holy Spirit on Pentecost. After Pentecost, God continued to establish his covenant with Jews who believed in Jesus as the

GOD'S TWO WAYS OF ESTABLISHING HIS COVENANT

Christ, the Son of the living God, *and* their children after them in their generations.

God also began to establish and continue his covenant with Gentiles who believed in Jesus *and* with their children after them. God still establishes and continues his covenant with believers and our children today. Therefore, in Reformed circles we often speak of our "covenantal children," "covenantal homes," and "covenantal schools." In fact, the high school I attended is called Covenant Christian High School.

But second, when Jesus gave his great commission to go into all the world and make disciples and then filled his apostles with the Holy Spirit on Pentecost, God began to extend the reach of his covenant into the whole world *through missions.* This is one of the things that distinguishes the new covenant from the old. This is one of the characteristic marks of the new covenant: God opening the doors of his covenant to all the nations of the world and sending the ambassadors of Christ over land and sea to announce the good news and gather the elect into Zion.

God established his covenant primarily with Gentiles after the age of the apostles as the gospel spread in all directions. God establishes his covenant with people of every nation, tribe, and tongue today through the thousands of missionaries who are preaching Christ near and far. Therefore, we need to learn in Reformed circles to speak also of our "covenantal mission fields" and "covenantal evangelism work" because God establishes his covenant not only among the children of believers but also in the outside world.

This is very important to understand for our Christian practice and life. There are two demands laid upon us by the Lord regarding the extension of his covenant in the New

Testament. We sometimes seem to think that our chief calling, if not our only calling, with respect to the extension of God's covenant is to train up our children in the way that they should go in the home, school, and church. That is indeed an extremely important calling that I would never want to minimize as a father of five. I consider my calling to teach and nurture our children in the home exceedingly important, and it does tend to dominate my day-to-day life. But I also insist, on the basis of Scripture, that we have another equally important calling in respect to the extension of God's covenant: the calling of missions.

What would be your answer if someone asked you what your calling is regarding the covenant? Many of us Reformed people would think only of our duty to teach our children in the home, make sure they learn their catechism lessons, and send them to a Christian school. But we ought also to mention our duty to love our neighbor outside the church and to present Christ to him or her when the opportunity arises.

We must learn to look inwardly and outwardly from our place in the church. We may not neglect either of these. They are equally important. There are churches that have become so outward focused that they neglect the catechizing of the children of the church and eventually see those children leave. But there are also many churches that are so inward focused that they seriously neglect the evangelizing of the lost, and they hardly ever see anyone join the church from the outside. They hardly ever see an adult baptism.

Both of these imbalanced perspectives are wrong. If the church of which we are a member puts all the attention on outreach to the neglect of the children of believers, we must call for change to remedy that situation. But if our church puts almost all the attention on the instruction of the children of believers, we must seek to kindle an awareness and zeal for outreach.

Our Covenantal Mission Mandate

Since the demand of the new covenant that we go and make disciples in all nations comes first of all to ministers of the gospel, I take a moment to address my brothers in the ministry. We ought to ask ourselves whether we are willing to count the cost of going into the world to preach the gospel and to be an instrument in the hands of God to gather the lost into his covenant. God is pleased to use the foolishness of the preaching of the cross by weak men like us to save those who believe (1 Cor. 1:21–29), to establish his covenant with them. God has called us to engage in this task of preaching near and far, inside and outside the church. God may call you to be a missionary, either in the nation of your upbringing or overseas in a foreign culture. What factors will you consider in connection with that call? No doubt, many things must be considered. But we still need to ask ourselves whether we are willing to count the cost of accepting that call and going far away to preach the gospel.

Would you be willing to sell your earthly belongings and leave your native land and way of life to move to a place where the sights and smells are very different and strange? To leave the covenantal community, perhaps in which you were born and raised and in which you have all your family and friends, in order to be involved in the establishment of new covenantal communities in other nations? To leave behind the life of the churches and schools that you love so dearly, the sporting events and Christmas concerts, the Easter choir programs and summer youth conventions, the work you consider so important at the ecclesiastical assemblies, and the warm fellowship you enjoy at the ministers' retreats and the officebearers' conferences? To bid farewell to your family and friends, your mother and father, your sister and brother, even as they weep to see you go? Jesus tells us: "He that loveth father or mother more than me is not worthy of me: and he that loveth son or daughter more than me is not worthy of me. And he that taketh not his cross, and followeth after me, is not worthy of me" (Matt. 10:37–38).

I ask these questions as one who missed all these things and more during the years that we were abroad in the Philippines. I ask these questions to myself too, as one who does not know whether the Lord will call me to go abroad again someday and do it all over again. Perhaps for us who are intimately connected with the history, people, schools, and way of life of our Reformed denominations, the call to leave it all behind and move to some exotic place in Asia or Africa, or even to some far-off corner in North America, feels particularly hard to do.

For us, it was hard to leave behind and lose close contact with our church and school communities and our friends and family in North America. It was hard to let go of sending our children to the Christian schools that we would most prefer. It was hard to move so far away from the official and unofficial gatherings for worship in our denomination. But although it was hard at first, the Lord, as he always does, turned it to our advantage and blessed us richly. You cannot clearly see those blessings before you go to the mission field. You see them after you have gone.

One of the greatest joys, of course, is to participate in the formation, fellowship, and worship of new covenantal communities in other cultures that God establishes through your labors as a missionary. To teach and preach the Scriptures to people of a nation that formerly did not know God…To sing the psalms, hymns, and spiritual songs of the Lord with believers and their seed who have a different color of skin than you do and a different mother tongue…To enjoy spiritual fellowship with them around tables laden with bowls of hot rice and delicious native dishes…I recall with fondness many unique and wonderful opportunities that the Lord gave me.

I was invited once to preach to a man and his family in his home in Manila. After enjoying the delicious meal he made for us, I opened and expounded the grand truths of the book of Romans for about an hour, then answered questions. What a delight! On another occasion, on the island of Leyte, we went from house to house in the poor village to visit the families of a group of believers. We read Scripture in the Tagalog language and prayed with them. What a thrill! Many more experiences could be listed. But the point is that there are great joys in store for those who go and serve the Lord in missions.

Some of you will never receive a call to be a missionary. Some of you will receive a call but will not be convinced that the Lord wills for you to go. Even so, you have a calling to reach out to the lost in your neighborhood, town, and vicinity. Therefore, you ruling elders who are reading this who have the oversight of your pastor must make sure that you not only allow your minister to engage in evangelism but encourage and enable him to do so. May God give fruit on your local outreach work and use it to lead men and women who grew up outside the covenant into the covenant.

Finally, if the great commission is directed chiefly to ministers, that does not mean there is no calling for the rest of the people of God. "Let your light so shine before men, that they may see your good works, and glorify your Father which is in heaven"

(Matt. 5:16). May it be said of you that you were outstanding examples of witnessing, "for from you sounded out the word of the Lord...so that we need not to speak anything" (1 Thess. 1:8).[4]

In Summary

The great commission and outpouring of the Holy Spirit on Pentecost marked the end of the age when God established his covenant in one way within the confines of one nation. It marked the beginning of this last age when God is fulfilling his promise to make Abraham a "father of many nations" (Gen. 17:4–5). In an earlier chapter, we considered this promise of God to Abraham. *Before* God uttered the promise to establish his covenant with believers and their seed in their generations (v. 7), he first declared that he would make his covenant with Abraham *as the father of many nations*.[5] God meant that Abraham would be the spiritual father of believers in Christ from all nations under heaven. God would multiply his seed like the stars of heaven, the sand on the seashore, and the dust of the

---

[4] See appendix 1 for a treatment of this passage of Scripture.

[5] Bruinsma mentions the promise to believers and their seed and asserts: "The truth of God's covenant teaches us that God will cause His church to grow from within the confines of that church by means of the generations born to believing parents." He adds: "There is another marvelous truth revealed in Genesis 17 that too often is overlooked. We read these words of God to Abraham in verses 4 and 5: 'As for me, behold, my covenant is with thee, and thou shalt be a father of many nations. Neither shall thy name any more be called Abram, but thy name shall be Abraham; for a father of many nations have I made thee.' Not only did God promise to establish a relationship of fellowship and friendship with Abraham and his seed, but God also told Abraham that in him all the nations of the earth would come to share in that fellowship and love of God." Bruinsma, "Defining Missions," 91.

GOD'S TWO WAYS OF ESTABLISHING HIS COVENANT

earth. For the purpose of God from the beginning of time was always to establish his covenant with the world of men, though not with every man.

Our Lord said: "As the Father knoweth me, even so know I the Father: and I lay down my life for the sheep. And other sheep I have, which are not of this fold: them also I must bring, and they shall hear my voice; and there shall be one fold, and one shepherd" (John 10:15-16). Jesus laid down his life for God's sheep, for those of "this fold" (the Jews) and for "other sheep" who were not of that fold (Gentiles).

He now prays at God's right hand that those who are still outside the covenantal fold will "hear his voice" in the preaching of the gospel and will come to him, so "that they all may be one; as thou, Father, art in me, and I in thee, that they also may be one in us" (17:20-21). This is the mission of Christ: to send preachers to declare his word not only within the fold but also out in the world, and thereby to bring all his sheep together into the one fold of God's covenant following one Shepherd.

When we use the word *covenant*, let us not assume that it is synonymous with the promise of God to us and our children but remember that it is the bond of friendship that God wills to establish with that richly diverse body of human beings whom Christ redeemed. When we memorize Genesis 17:7 and treasure that verse deep in our hearts, let us also memorize verses 4 to 5 and treasure it just as deeply. When we teach about the recipients of the covenant in our catechism classes and sermons, let us not forget that God changed Abram's name to Abraham, "father of a multitude," for in this last age of history in which we are privileged to live, he draws a multitude of believers from every people, tribe, nation, and language under heaven into his everlasting covenant of grace.

To summarize: God establishes his covenant with his people through missions, as he apparently did with my ancestors in the medieval Netherlands. He continues establishing his covenant through them with others in two directions: first, with their elect seed after them in the lines of continuing generations, and second, with the elect who sit in the darkness of the world. Therefore, the church must develop a culture not only for the pious and religious education of the children of believers, but also for the zealous and active evangelizing of the world. We turn to this subject next.

STUDY QUESTIONS

1. What comes to mind when you hear the verse: "For the promise is unto you, and to your children, and to all that are afar off, even as many as the Lord our God shall call" (Acts 2:39)? What does this mean for our children? Who are "all that are afar off"?

2. Is it correct to say that God has two ways of establishing his covenant in the New Testament? Why or why not?

3. Is it proper to say that the education of our children and the evangelization of the lost are both demands of the covenant in the New Testament?

4. Should ministers be more willing to accept a call to a mission field than to stay in their current church or go to another established church? Explain.

5

A CULTURE FOR MISSIONS IN THE COVENANTAL COMMUNITY

Back in 2008, when I was still in seminary, I first heard the interesting expression in the title of this chapter. I was sitting in the pew of a church in West Michigan at a missions conference, writing notes as Pastor Jason Kortering (1936–2020) spoke on the subject of the need for special training for the work of missions.

Kortering was born and raised in the same denomination as I was and served God faithfully for many years in the ministry of the gospel. He not only served as a pastor in a number of well-established, multi-generational churches in North America, but he also spent the 1990s laboring in a young church of many first-generation believers in Singapore. That involved him in a kind of evangelistic work that was much less common in the churches he had served in the U.S. It also gave him opportunity to go on several mission trips to other Asian countries, including Myanmar, India, and the Philippines. He was passionate about missions. The passion came out in his preaching and writing. In the first part of his speech on that September night in 2008, he said that Christ gives the gift of missionaries out of the life of the church, and therefore we must create a "culture for missions" in our churches and schools.

Creating a Culture for Missions

That idea of the need to create a "culture for missions" in the covenantal community was an intriguing notion to me as a young aspirant to the ministry, and it has stuck with me ever since I first heard it. I read an almost identical expression from another source recently, a collection of articles written by a conservative, evangelistic Reformed minister in the heart of New York City. He said to the readers of *Christian Renewal* magazine:

> We must create a culture of evangelism in our congregations...This starts with the expectation that every church should grow and reproduce not only biologically but with conversions...Every church is to be a missionary church spreading the Gospel in its community and seeking the conversion of the lost there. This will best occur when it occurs organically in the life of her members.[1]

What would it look like if the covenantal community had a *culture for missions*? I have been pondering that question now for well over a decade. I think it is quite clear from the many articles, books, conferences, podcasts, and blogs devoted

---

1 Paul T. Murphy, *A Humble Effort to Promote Local Evangelism*, 8. This book was originally a set of articles which began on February 25, 2009, in the *Christian Renewal* magazine.

to missions that there has been a growing zeal for missions in conservative Reformed churches in the twenty-first century. I have witnessed signs of greater zeal for missions in my own small, conservative Reformed denomination, even as we passed through the most tumultuous period of trouble and controversy in my lifetime. I have no intention to deny or minimize the good developments regarding evangelism that the Lord has produced in my and other Reformed denominations.

Nevertheless, I think there is still something missing. We need a culture that sees the instruction of our children in the home, school, and church not as a calling that is separate and unrelated to missions, but one that supports and increases our mission to bring the gospel to the world, locally and globally. We need a way of thinking that does not, consciously or unconsciously, compartmentalize missions into a small corner of the mind as a calling for a few brave missionaries and the few people who get put on our church's evangelism committee. We need to renew our minds if we think that missions has very little to do with us and our children, or with our local church.

A certain pastor in my denomination was once asked: "How does your church witness to the community?" He reportedly answered that they had a sign out front. The neighbors can see the sign. They know that we are here. That was enough in his mind. I agree that there should be a good sign in front of our church telling the community who we are. But the idea that having a sign more or less fulfills our duty to bear witness to the community illustrates the unacceptable attitude about the covenant and missions that prevailed in the past and that still needs to change.

GO INTO ALL THE WORLD

A Culture for Teaching the Children of Believers

The need for a culture for missions does not preclude the need for a robust culture for the catechizing and educating of the children of believers in the church. On the contrary, it assumes and depends on such a culture. A church could throw huge amounts of energy and money into community outreach and evangelism projects, while providing little more than nursery, fun arts and crafts, puppet shows, and kid songs to the children of their own members. Parents do not take their children into the worship service to listen to the sermon and sing with the congregation. There is little to no rigorous instruction in the history of the Bible and the doctrines of the faith. There is a lack of spiritual attention for the children of believers. That would be a grave mistake. A culture for missions must never arise *in the place of* the vigorous instruction of the children of the covenant in the preaching on Sundays and in the catechism classes.

Nor ought we to downgrade the Christian school movement in order to create a culture for missions. There are many professing Christians who do not promote the establishment and use of Christian schools by Christian parents. They do not believe, evidently, that our duty as members of God's covenant to teach our children Jehovah's truth and raise them up as Christians in community with other Christians summons us to establish good Christian schools where all things are taught within the framework of a biblical worldview. They seem to have a kind of unholy contentment with the public schools, where their children mingle with the children of the world as they learn science, art, music, history, health, and the other subjects from the perspective of a secular worldview. This neglect is part of the reason why the youth of America are steadily flowing out of the churches and why more and more young people in America claim to have no religion.[2]

There has long been a belief in some Reformed circles that establishing Christian schools and keeping our children separate from the world is a mistake. Jesus taught us to be in the world but not of the world (John 17:15–16). Therefore, according to this view, we ought not to isolate our children from the children of the world in Christian schools. We ought to send them to the public schools where they can shine as lights in the world, witness to the children of unbelievers, and be a force for good in society.

But this is a serious mistake. We must remember that the whole educational enterprise is spiritual and religious in nature. Schools do not merely teach the cold, hard facts of nature, math, and history. Schools also teach, or at least assume, philosophies that interpret those facts. Schools also teach or assume in their teaching worldviews that influence the way children think about God; the origin, development, and future of the universe; and moral right and wrong.

When Jesus taught us to be in the world but not of the world, he did not mean we should put our lambs on the bus each day with the children of the world and send them out of the sheepfold of the covenantal community into a den of lions. He did not mean we ought to send out our tender and vulnerable children into the world with the hope that they will exert

---

[2] "There is a fundamental flaw in government-controlled education of children. The *government* controls the content of what is taught in the schools. Parents have no voice in the education of their own children… Allowing the children of God's covenant to be taught academically by unbelievers, by those who despise God and his commandments, is like giving our lambs to the wolves!" Bruinsma, *Life in the Covenant*, 131.

a Christian influence on the lost sheep out there. On the contrary, we must strive each day to protect our little ones from the evil influences of ungodly educational systems and lead them daily to see, hear, and follow the good Shepherd in the home, school, and church until they reach an age of discretion.

Are there Christian children in public schools who are letting their light shine by taking a stand against the evils there? I know that there are, but that takes nothing away from the parents' calling to provide a Christian education to their children. Moreover, there are many more children in the public schools who are losing whatever elements of the Christian faith they were taught and abandoning that faith for the supposed wisdom of our secular age that they are learning at school.

In summary, a culture for missions does not preclude the establishment and maintenance of good Christian schools. Nor does it involve sending our children out into society as little missionaries to let their light shine to the unbelieving children of the neighborhood.

A Culture for Missions in Our Homes

What, then, am I calling for when I speak of the need to create a culture for missions in the covenantal community? I am calling out to my fellow believers to recognize that we need to increase our outward-focused zeal for missions, both in theory and in practice, until it matches the level of our inward-focused zeal for our children and grandchildren. I am calling for a change of mind, heart, and life:

1. *A change of mind* so that we grasp and affirm the theology of Scripture that God establishes his covenant

in two places, not just with us and our children in the lines of continued generations, but also with all who are afar off whom he will call, and that he wills to use us to do so, not only as parents to our children but also as his witnesses to our neighbors.

2. *A change of heart* so that in our interactions with strangers and neighbors we are less and less ashamed of the gospel of Christ, who loved us unto the death of the cross, and more and more filled with a love that longs to see God gather others into his covenant, including our unbelieving neighbors and the heathen in other nations who are without God in the world.

3. *A change of life* so that we begin to look more and more for the opportunities that God gives us to support local and world missions and for ways to hold forth the word of life to our non-Christian neighbors through our church's evangelism efforts and our own personal witness.

Is there a culture for missions in our homes? I ask us to examine whether our "covenantal homes" are purely inward-focused or also outward-focused. Does the light shine only within the four walls of our house or also through the windows of our house, as it were, out into the world around us? Do we ignore our neighbors and mind our own business, or do we interact with the people around us in the desire to tell them about the hope that is in us through Christ? A covenantal home in which father and mother focus entirely on their own children needs to look outside the windows and remember that God wills to establish his covenant with the whole world of the people he loves.

To illustrate what a culture of missions looks like in the home, I can describe how I envision it and seek to implement it in my own home. My home is like other homes in many ways. There are routines of work, school, church, catechism, sports, meals, vacations, and more. But we strive to avoid having a narrow-minded concern for our own family, friends, church, and school. We try to devote thought, attention, and prayer to the lost souls in the neighborhood and the church in all nations too. We try to raise our children in such a way as to impress on their minds and hearts the truth that God sends the church into the world on a mission to shine the light of the gospel.

As parents, we talk about that mission of the church around the dinner table at family devotions. Maybe in our Bible reading we have just read a passage from the Old Testament prophets that speaks of God's promise to gather in the Gentiles from the ends of the earth, or a passage from the book of Acts that describes the missionary journeys of the apostle Paul. At one point when I was working on this book, we read the epistle of Paul to the Ephesians in our family devotions. I was struck again by what he wrote in chapters 2 and 3 about the extension of God's covenant into all nations.

I don't know how many times I have looked up Ephesians 2 in connection with the great truths of total depravity and salvation by grace alone through faith alone (vv. 1–10). But I think there have not been nearly as many times when I have focused on the great truths that follow, that those who were once "without Christ, being aliens from the commonwealth of Israel, and strangers from the covenants of promise, having no hope, and without God in the world" have been brought "nigh by the blood of Christ...who hath made both one, and hath broken down the middle wall of partition between us," so that

A CULTURE FOR MISSIONS

through the work of missions in their midst, they are "no more strangers and foreigners, but fellowcitizens with the saints, and of the household of God" (vv. 12–19). Paul speaks of the mystery of Christ that had been revealed to him, "that the Gentiles should be fellow heirs, and of the same body, and partakers of his promise in Christ by the gospel" (3:6). We parents do well at our family devotions to take time with passages like these to instill in our children an understanding of God's grand purpose to extend his covenant into all the world through missions.

Believing parents who understand and care about God's mission to save his lost sheep in all nations will take the opportunity to inform their children about the current mission fields of their denomination or evangelism efforts of their local church. As the children grow older, the spiritual conversations, including those about missions, will carry over from the dinner table into the living room after supper. The father will not have a negative attitude about the efforts of the church to call men away from established congregations to the mission field. Nor will he criticize the amount of money the churches spend on missions. Rather, he will speak positively and excitedly about missions. The children will come to realize the importance of missions. You talk most about the things you care about most. It is important to regularly ask ourselves what we care about most.

Christian parents also need to talk with their children about the neighbors who live next door or down the street. But they do not just expose the faults of those neighbors and bemoan all the evil things they do: their Sabbath desecration, their bad language, their laziness, their atheism, or whatever. They do not just criticize and condemn them for how messed up their lives are from divorce, drugs, alcohol, gambling, poverty, and so on. If we stop at that, we are no better than the Pharisees who reviled the publicans and sinners with whom Jesus would eat.

Rather, parents who want to raise their children to care about the mission of Christ to seek and to save the lost will talk with them about how we might reach our neighbors, how to witness to them, how to show Christ to them as the Savior of sinners. But they don't just talk about witnessing to the neighbors. They *actually* witness to them, so that their children see in them an example to follow.

Christian parents also need to pray in front of their children for the church's missions and their own personal witness. They pray out loud for their unbelieving neighbors that God will call them to Christ, if he wills. They pray by name for the missionaries whom they know and for the nations in which they labor. They do not just pray for God to raise up more pastors to supply the pulpits of the many churches in the denomination. They do not just pray that God will move more young men and women to pursue a career of teaching in the Christian schools to supply the lack of teachers. But they also pray for God to call men to be missionaries and to go into the world preaching the gospel to those afar off.

Their children hear those prayers and come to realize the importance of missions. And if God would answer those prayers by calling one of their *own* sons to be a missionary on a foreign field, or one of their *own* daughters to be a missionary's wife, Christian parents would not be sorrowful and dejected. Rather, they would rejoice that God was pleased to use one of their own children for this all-important work. We need to ask ourselves the question: do we have a culture for missions in our homes?

A Culture for Missions in Our Schools

We also need to ask ourselves whether we have a culture for missions in our Christian schools. I pointed out earlier that we ought not send our children to the public schools as little missionaries, but educate them according to the demands of the covenant in Christian schools. When it comes to the education of our children, we must come out from among them and be separate and touch not the unclean thing (2 Cor. 6:17).

But we must also avoid the danger on the other side: when we isolate our children from the world in our own schools, we face the constant temptation to become insulated from the world, to have little to no contact with the world in the areas in which we live, and thus to make little to no impact on the world in terms of the gospel. We feel safe within the walls of our homes and schools, and we view the world out there as nothing more than the spiritually perilous domain of Satan that we ought to have nothing to do with, especially as society becomes more and more wicked.

David Engelsma warns against the danger of world flight. He gives a defense of a liberal arts education to prepare our children "to live in this world, really *in this world*, in all its different spheres."[3] I agree with that warning (John 17:15). I also issue the

---

3 David J. Engelsma, *Reformed Education: The Christian School as the Demand of the Covenant* (Jenison, MI: Reformed Free Publishing Association, 2000), 41. He writes: "We are not free altogether from the temptation of the world-flight mentality" (42). This mentality "considers the physical world and its institutions an evil and concludes that a Christian must get out of the world as much as possible. It advocates physical separation from the world, shunning normal earthly life" (49). Some people esteem "the Christian school mainly because it keeps the children separate from the public school children" (49–50). Engelsma defends the teaching of a liberal arts education in our schools from a Reformed perspective with the goal of preparing the child of God to live in the world "in every area of life with all his powers as God's friend-servant, loving God and serving God in all of his earthly life with all his abilities" (84).

warning against world flight, not so much in defense of a liberal arts education, but in promotion of a culture for missions in the schools. The Christian school must prepare the children of the covenant to live in this world, really in this world, as *witnesses* of Christ in every sphere of society. The Christian school must impress on the children of believers that we may not run out of the world, because God has given the church a mission to the world that will continue until Jesus comes again.

When we separate our children in our own schools, we also face the constant threat of allowing a self-centered mentality to take root in our hearts. Then we run the risk of letting our school become the only thing that is precious and important to us. What we care about is our school. What we pour all our time and energy into is our school.

But we must not be so focused on *our* children that we find no room in our hearts for God's mission to gather *his* children out of the world into his covenant. We can wax eloquent about the beauty of the covenantal home and the preciousness of the covenantal school. But if we have no love in our hearts for the lost sinners around us, we are out of harmony with the will of God, like Jonah who delighted in Jehovah's tender mercy toward Israel but was opposed to God bestowing the grace of salvation on the wretched heathen sinners of Nineveh.

If our children grow up with little interest in the extension of the covenant to others outside the church through missions and evangelism, that did not happen because we separated them from the world and educated them in our own schools. But that happened because we allowed a self-centered and self-preserving attitude to rule in our schools. The problem is not that we gave them a Christian education; the problem is that we did not weave into that Christian education our calling to reach out to the unreached world and shine the gospel into the nations in our own backyard and afar off. The problem is not that we shielded them from the ungodly influences of evolutionism and transgenderism that run rampant in the public schools so that they became sheltered and naïve; the problem is that we were more concerned about preserving our way of life and ensuring the earthly success of our children than we were about the salvation of God's lost people who are still outside the church.

When that is the case, we are not that different from the middle-class parents of the world who want to ensure the earthly success of their children. What is more important to us, that our children get a good education and do well in this earthly life, or that they shine as lights in the darkness and learn to speak boldly and humbly about Jesus to an unbelieving world?

Psalm 127 teaches us that we must trust in the Lord with all our hearts as we build our covenantal homes, and that applies to the schools that we parents establish together too. Our children are a heritage from the Lord, and the fruit of the womb is his reward. Happy is the man who has a quiver full of sharp arrows. The psalm does not proclaim the happiness of the man who merely has *children*, or the man who has *healthy* and *successful* children, or even the man whose children stay in the church and contribute to the life of the covenantal community. But happy is the man who has a quiver full of children who are "as arrows in the hand of a mighty man" (v. 4). Our goal in building our covenantal homes and educating our children in the Christian school should be to raise up children who are sharp and useful like arrows, who are ready to be shot forth into the world, who are ready to "speak with the enemies in the gate" (v. 5), not ashamed of the gospel of Christ, but confident in God and brave to confess Christ before men.

A number of years ago, when I was researching the history of missions in the Christian Reformed Church, I came across a book that made a very interesting remark. One of the motives that led our Dutch Reformed forefathers to establish Christian schools in America in the nineteenth century was that the children of the covenant would be well prepared to live in the world *as witnesses of Christ*.[4]

That is exactly my point here. Do our schools fill our children with knowledge to prepare them to succeed in their future career? Do they teach our children how to think and live in service to God within the covenantal community? That's all good. But they must also consciously prepare our children to live in the world as witnesses of Christ. That's a culture for missions in a covenantal school.

When I imagine a school that tries to instruct the children of believers to see the importance of missions, I picture in my mind an association of parents and grandparents, a school board, a principal, and teachers who are conscious of the great importance of missions and who intentionally seek to instill in the children an appreciation for God's mission to bring the gospel to the whole world. Teachers emphasize that the goal of their instruction is not just to help the students get a good job, but to shine as lights in the world; not by becoming social and political activists who try to establish a kingdom of God on earth by Christianizing all of society, but by learning to walk and talk as citizens of the heavenly kingdom of Christ in every sphere of life and thus to let their light shine before men.

---

4 See John Harold Bratt, *The Missionary Enterprise of the Christian Reformed Church in America* (Th.D. dissertation, Union Theological Seminary, Virginia, 1955), 11.

A CULTURE FOR MISSIONS

In the classroom, teachers not only teach the children what the Bible says but also train them to speak about their faith with those who do not know Christ in order to prepare them for the day when they will brush shoulders with unbelievers in the workplace. A colleague of mine suggested that the Christian schools could even incorporate into their curriculum specific classes to train our children how to share the gospel and defend their faith to non-Christians (for example, an evangelism, apologetics, or worldview class). When teaching history, a teacher could take the opportunity to make connections to the history of missions. When teaching geography, a teacher could take the opportunity to make connections to current mission fields.

I recall a teacher in a West Michigan grade school once asking me to come to his classroom to talk about the Philippines when he was teaching a unit on Asia in one of his classes. What a great way to show the children that these far-off, exotic places that they're learning about are real places where God sends missionaries! My fellow missionaries and I were also asked on our furloughs to give mission-field presentations to Christian schools. We always considered that an important invitation and a way to help instill in the children of the covenant a sense of the importance of missions.

Chapel services could also be devoted to missions. I remember a speech by a minister to a mass meeting of young people (when I was one of them) that told us about persecuted churches in faraway lands. It made a big impression on me. Speakers can tell the tales of past missionaries too. There are no doubt many other ways we can instruct, promote, and awaken in our children the importance of missions in our schools. God will use such efforts to shape and fashion young men to be missionaries and young women to go with them as their wives.

A Culture for Missions in Our Churches

I am not aware of a church that does no mission work whatsoever. Churches do missions. But not all churches have a culture for missions. Churches that have a culture for missions are those that are active *to the best of their ability* in training, sending, and supporting missionaries in a variety of foreign and domestic fields. They are churches led by pastors, elders, and governing bodies that are *genuinely fervent in prayer* for the Lord to raise up laborers whom the church may send out into the world. They are churches that have professors of theology in their seminary who *emphasize constantly and in a variety of ways* the twofold duty of the preacher of the gospel to feed the flock *and* to evangelize the lost, to feed the lambs *and* to go into all the world in missions. They are churches whose *ordained ministers* know Christ as their Lord and Savior who loved them and gave himself for them and who long to make Christ known not only in established churches but also in heathen lands afar off, wherever he sends them and whatever the cost may be.

Do you have such a culture for missions in your churches? What does that look like?

There is a culture for missions in the church if the pastor prays for missions almost if not every Sunday in his congregational prayers; if his ministry involves not only the baptism of the infants of believers and the catechizing of those children as they grow up, but also the discipling of new converts in catechism classes specially tailored for them with a view to their baptism; if he preaches Christ crucified and risen as our only hope in life and death and exhorts his congregation regularly to show forth that salvation from day to day in their personal witness; if he instructs his congregation often about the idea and calling of missions as the Scriptures lay it out in many places in the Old and New Testaments; if he practices what he preaches by being heavily involved in the work of the evangelism committee of his church and by witnessing personally to his own neighbors.

My fellow pastors, do we witness personally to our next-door neighbors? We ought to lead by example by witnessing to the unchurched people on our blocks, in our towns, and on our roads.

In Reformed circles, we generally maintain that the office of evangelist that existed in the early church (Eph. 4:11) has ceased to exist, just as the office of apostle has. But a church with a culture for missions does not put all the emphasis on the fact that this office has ceased to exist. Rather, such a church emphasizes that the office of evangelist has merged into the office of pastor and is an essential element of that office (2 Tim. 4:5). We pastors must do the work of an evangelist! Do we? You elders must support your pastor in this work. Do you?

In the churches of which I am a part, we pastors are expected to preach two sermons to the congregation every Sunday, to teach catechism to most if not all of the children of the church, to lead some if not all of the Bible studies, to visit most if not all of the sick and widows, to counsel those in emotional, spiritual, and marital distress, and often to serve on denominational committees. In this context, the work of evangelism is often considered less important. If there is extra time and if the pastor wants to do it, great. But if he is too busy, he must focus on his duties in the church. That is wrong thinking.

The pastor must do the work of an evangelist. That means he must be involved in bringing the gospel (the evangel) to those outside the church in which he labors. His elders must not hinder that but encourage it. They may have to provide assistance in some of his other work so that he has time for it. They may have to rethink their expectations for his workload to ensure that he has time to preach the word at a homeless shelter on a weeknight, lead a Bible study at a local college with interested young people, lead services at a nursing home on a Sunday, hand out gospel literature at town events in the summertime, have coffee with neighbors to discuss the Christian faith, or prepare special catechism classes for new believers.

In my younger years (1980s and 1990s), I do not believe there was a culture for missions in the churches of which I was a baptized member. There were some mission fields and faithful missionaries. But in my memory, there was very little emphasis on the great commission. At least I must confess that I personally paid little attention to missions until my seminary years.

I believe that in the past couple of decades, though, there has been a growing zeal for missions, not only in the churches in which I live and labor but also in other Reformed churches. That interest must continue to grow, and it will as we grasp with our minds and hearts that the building of the spiritual house of the Lord in this dispensation is a two-pronged endeavor. There must be a culture for the Christian home and school on the one hand, but also a culture for missions on the other.

A CULTURE FOR MISSIONS

STUDY QUESTIONS

1. Do you have a culture for missions in your home? If not, what is hindering you? What can you start doing today to teach your children the importance of missions?

2. Why is it wrong to send our children to public schools in order to expose them to other worldviews and teach them to be Christian witnesses in the world?

3. What can you do in your local Christian school (as a supporter or as a teacher) to promote a proper culture for missions?

4. Pastors, do you "do the work of an evangelist" in your communities and neighborhoods? If not, what has to change in your workload so that you can spend more time in this vital part of our calling?

6

GO INTO ALL THE WORLD, BUT BE YE SEPARATE!

When I was growing up in my Reformed denomination, one of the great truths that was impressed upon my soul as a child of the covenant was what we often call "the antithesis."[1] The word *antithesis* contains the prefix *anti*, which means "against." The word *antichrist* has the same prefix. There is Christ, and there are antichrists. An antichrist is one who is against Christ. Similarly, there is a thesis, and there is an antithesis. The antithesis is the one who stands against the thesis.

God, who is light, is the thesis, together with his elect in Christ with whom he establishes his covenant. Satan, the lord of darkness, is the antithesis, together with the wicked world of the reprobate who are under his dominion. Satan is against God. But God and Satan are not two equal powers who oppose each other, for God is sovereign over Satan, and his victory through Christ is absolutely sure.

But the word *antithesis*, practically speaking, became shorthand for our calling with respect to the world of darkness:

---

[1] See Herman Hanko, *For Thy Truth's Sake* (Grandville, MI: Reformed Free Publishing Association, 2000), 176–198.

that we must stand against the world, that is, those who are the enemies of our God. We must come out from among them and be separate and touch not the unclean thing, as the Lord has said (2 Cor. 6:17). What was impressed upon me by this word *antithesis*, then, was that our whole calling as God's covenantal people with respect to the world in which we live could be summed up as standing *against* the wicked, fighting *against* them as our spiritual foes, fleeing *from* them when they tempt us to sin, staying *out* of their dens of iniquity like the movie theater, the bar, and the casino, and making no friendships with them. It was indeed emphasized that we must live godly lives *in* the world in every sphere of life. But it was not emphasized that we must go *into* the world, whether as preachers or ordinary believers, and bring the gospel to those who sit in darkness.

God makes clear in many passages of Scripture that he wills us to go into the world and shine as lights in the darkness, bringing the gospel and doing good to all men, holding forth the word of life and being a neighbor to those beaten, bruised, and left for dead. No, we do not have a calling to Christianize the world in the postmillennial sense of the word. We know that the world is not going to get better and better but that the antichrist will rise before Christ returns, and darkness will fall over the whole world. We know that there will not be a golden age of peace and prosperity here on earth, and that it is not up to us to bring such a thing to pass by our preaching and activism.

Nevertheless, God calls us to live as his covenantal people in the world, as the salt of the earth, and that includes the *positive* calling to go into the world and testify of Christ by our words and deeds, whether as ordained ministers or as lay Christians. How then do we obey these two callings with respect to the world as God's covenantal people, the one negative and the other positive: come out from among them and be ye separate, but go into the world and shine in the darkness?

Israel in the Midst of the Nations

Let us be clear that both these callings are based on and flow out of the Holy Scriptures. In the Old Testament, God made clear when he established his covenant with Abraham, Isaac, and Jacob, and later with the nation of Israel, that they were to live in spiritual separation from the ungodly nations around them. God placed his people within the borders of the Promised Land. God placed an antithesis, in the sense of a wall of hostility, between them and the world, and Israel would dwell in safety alone (Deut. 33:28). Do not give your daughters to the sons of the Canaanites in marriage, God said to them. But destroy their altars and break down their images. Do not have fellowship with the Moabites, God said. But remain in the land that the Lord has given you as an inheritance. For you are a holy people unto the Lord your God (7:1–7).

In fact, God kept Israel *physically* separate from the other nations in the Old Testament. He was teaching Israel as a parent teaches his children. A parent in his desire to teach his children what is right and wrong will often isolate them physically from what is spiritually dangerous, for example, by installing a filter on the family computer so that the children will not even be exposed to the perverse content on the internet. Similarly, God isolated Israel physically from the other nations in the Old Testament. He established a geographic border around the land, in part to teach that he had given them that land flowing with milk and honey as a free inheritance in his sovereign electing love, but in part to teach that they ought not to wander outside the kingdom of God into the paths of the heathen.

God also called Israel to fight physical battles with sword and spear against those heathen nations and to drive them out of the land. He was teaching the reality of the great battle of the antithesis between good and evil in which they, too, must fight as God's covenantal people. Of course, Israel's failure to eradicate the Canaanites from the land coupled with the spiritually corrupt nature of the Israelites themselves drove them into those paths of the heathen anyway, and ultimately led to their apostasy and captivity in Babylon. But the point is that in the Old Testament, God called his people not only to spiritual separation but, as is evident from the geographic borders he established and the bloody wars he called them to fight, to physical separation from the world as well.

However, God showed already in the Old Testament that his people also have a positive calling with respect to the nations, for he promised Abraham that he would bless all the families of the earth in him (Gen. 12:3) and promised to send the Messiah for a covenant of the people and a light to the Gentiles (Isa. 42:6–7). In fact, God almost seemed to *send* Israel into those nations when he inspired the psalmist to exhort Israel to "declare his glory among the heathen, his wonders among all people…Say among the heathen that the Lord reigneth: the world also shall be established that it shall not be moved: he shall judge the people righteously" (Ps. 96:3, 10). Isaiah declared to his fellow Jews: "Ye are my witnesses, saith the Lord, and my servant whom I have chosen: that ye may know and believe me, and understand that I am he: before me there was no God formed, neither shall there be after me" (Isa. 43:10).

Yet if we study the Old Testament carefully, we do not find any commission from God with the clarity and scope of the commission Jesus gave to his disciples. God never called Israel to the tremendous task of bringing the gospel into all the nations of the world. That is partly why his call to Jonah was so startling to the prophet. You have not issued a call like this before, Jonah thought, and now you tell me to go outside the borders of the Promised Land and preach the gospel to the heathen in Nineveh! In the Old Testament, God called a few prophets to speak his word to the nations, but those were usually oracles of doom and destruction. He called Israel his witnesses, but they were a witness primarily by their existence in the midst of the nations as a people that worships Jehovah.

Come Out, Then Go In!

Major changes took place when Christ came. God poured out his Holy Spirit upon his church and stopped teaching his people through types and shadows. He now deals with us as spiritual adults (Gal. 4:1–7). He broke down the wall of separation between Israel and the Gentiles through the cross of Christ and opened the way for the nations to flow into Mount Zion (Isa. 2:2; Eph. 2:14). He removed the geographic border around his covenantal people. He stopped issuing commands to his covenantal people to shed the physical blood of the heathen. He has done away with those types and shadows, and he no longer calls us to be physically separate from the world.

Does God still call us to be spiritually separate from the world in the New Testament? He surely does. When God establishes his covenant with us in Christ today, whether in the lines of continued generations or through missions, he calls us to come out from among the ungodly.

> 14. Be ye not unequally yoked together with unbelievers: for what fellowship hath righteousness with unrighteousness? and what communion hath light with darkness?
> 15. And what concord hath Christ with Belial? or what part hath he that believeth with an infidel?
> 16. And what agreement hath the temple of God with idols? for ye are the temple of the living God; as God hath said, I will dwell in them, and walk in them; and I will be their God, and they shall be my people.
> 17. Wherefore come out from among them, and be ye separate, saith the Lord, and touch not the unclean thing; and I will receive you.
> 18. And will be a Father unto you, and ye shall be my sons and daughters, saith the Lord Almighty. (2 Cor. 6:14–18)

There are many texts that call us to live in spiritual separation from the wicked world, as the light in the midst of the darkness, not conformed to this world but transformed by the renewing of our minds, having no fellowship with the unfruitful works of darkness, rejecting the philosophies of man, keeping ourselves unspotted from the world, walking no longer as the heathen, and loving not the world or the things that are in the world (Matt. 5:13–16; Rom. 12:1–2; Eph. 5:1–14; Col. 2:4–10; James 1:27; 1 Pet. 4:1–4; 1 John 2:15).

Nevertheless, God in Christ also issued a clear and great commission to the church of the new covenant. He mandated us whom he has called out of the world to go into the world. God will not allow us to remain physically separate from the world in the New Testament, to hide our light under a bushel, as it were, inside our covenantal communities. God will not allow us to think that there is a boundary line around our covenantal homes, schools, and churches, and that we may not wander beyond the line. But God in Christ has made us the light of the world, a city on a hill that cannot be hid, and he calls us to be in the world, yet not of the world (Matt. 5:14–15; John 17:16).

God in this present age calls his covenantal people to plunge into the midst of the world. He calls us to cross cultural boundaries, whether by going overseas as a foreign missionary or talking over the fence to the Indian Hindu or Filipino Catholic or Canadian atheist who lives next door, all of which I have had opportunity to do in my life. God sends his covenantal people into the world to call those whom he has predestined to be his covenantal people out of that world.

In the book of Acts, we see Paul bringing the gospel to the Jew first, "to whom pertaineth the adoption, and the glory, and the covenants, and the giving of the law, and the service of God, and the promises; whose are the fathers, and of whom as concerning the flesh Christ came" (Rom. 9:4–5). But when the Jews rejected Jesus as the Christ, Paul brought the gospel outside the covenantal community to the Gentiles. As he said in Antioch of Pisidia: "Lo, we turn to the Gentiles. For so hath the Lord commanded us, saying, I have set thee to be a light of the Gentiles, that thou shouldest be for salvation unto the ends of the earth. And when the Gentiles heard this, they were glad, and glorified the word of the Lord: and as many as were ordained to eternal life believed" (Acts 13:46–48). Knowing that Christ has torn down the wall between Jews and Gentiles and sent us into the world to open the eyes of the blind and "to turn them from darkness to light, and from the power of Satan unto God, that they may receive forgiveness of sins and inheritance among them which are sanctified by faith" (26:18), Paul went outside the covenantal community and shone the light of the gospel to the heathen.

God calls us to do likewise.

But his calling is not the same for all of us. Some of us are pastors who have the calling to feed the flock of the congregation that has called us, to do evangelistic work in the neighborhood around us, and to stir up our congregations to participate in that work. Some are missionaries who are called to go outside the church and preach the gospel to the world, often in foreign nations with different cultures and customs, and to establish churches of believers and their seed. Some are professors of theology who are called to train men for the ministry, whether in a local church or on a mission field, and to instill in them a zeal for both. The rest of you are lay believers, men and women, with a wide variety of vocations that take some of you out of the home and even far away on business but keep some of you nearby, whether as a mother in the home or a father working from home. Some of you have jobs that involve much interaction with unbelievers, whereas others work with fellow believers.

Yet if we are believers in Jesus Christ and members of his church, we are God's covenantal people in the world who have this twofold calling to come out from among them and "maintain the antithesis" *and* to go into the midst of the world with the gospel. This is how and where the truths of the covenant, the antithesis, and the mission of the church all intersect.

GO INTO ALL THE WORLD, BUT BE YE SEPARATE

Getting Practical and Concrete

Let us apply this whole package of concepts to our lives. What will our lives look like as believers in Christ and members of God's covenant if we strive both to keep ourselves unspotted from the world *and* to share the gospel with the world?

In general, we will shine as lights in the world wherever we go. Christ tells us that we are the light of the world (Matt. 5:14). That is true of us as the church *and* as individual believers. That is true of us even though by nature we are nothing but darkness. It is true of us only because of Christ. He is the light of the world, first of all (John 8:12). He shines his light into our souls by his Holy Spirit through the preaching of the gospel from Sunday to Sunday. He lights our candles, so to speak, every Lord's day through the gospel of our salvation. He fires us up. He ignites us by his word, so that we will shine all week long. But he warns us not to hide our light under a bushel, as we are inclined to do by nature, whether in our hearts, homes, schools, or churches. Rather, he calls us to let our light so shine before men that they may see our good works and glorify our Father in heaven (Matt. 5:16).

Has Christ lit your candle? Has he kindled a fire in your heart through the gospel? What have you done with this little light of yours? We must not hide it inside our hearts or inside the confines of our homes and schools. We need to open up the shades and let our light shine out through the windows into the darkness of our neighborhoods! We need to carry that candle out the front door and let it shine before our neighbors when we're at the park with our kids or working out at the gym. We need to take it with us to work every day and let it shine there too. That means more than refraining from cursing and swearing on the jobsite. That goes without saying. But it means, too, that instead of cursing and swearing we speak about the things of God and Christ, about our faith and hope.

The call to maintain the antithesis does not preclude or forbid close interaction with the men and women of the world. We cannot have close fellowship and friendship with them, as long as they remain unbelievers. But we can and ought to have close interaction with them. We cannot be friends with them in the fullest sense of the word *friend*. But we can and ought to have some kind of relationship with them that involves discussions on the things that matter most in life: who God is, whether there is salvation for sinners, and what hope we have in death.

God calls you men who go to work every day to "study to be quiet, and to do your own business, and to work with your own hands" (1 Thess. 4:11). But that is not a call to avoid all meaningful conversation, to just get the job done and go home, for God also calls you to "shine as lights in the world; holding forth the word of life" (Phil. 2:15–16). The spirit of our age tells us that we should never talk about religion or politics at work unless we want to make things awkward. But the Holy Spirit tells us that we are a city on a hill that cannot be hidden and that we must let our light shine.

A man who is a friend of God in the bond of the covenant of grace must be different from his coworkers in many respects. He must not curse and swear as they do. He must not engage in foolish and filthy jesting about sex as they might do. He must not listen to the God-dishonoring and soul-harming hard rock music that they do, if he can avoid it. He must not complain as they do about their wages or work conditions. He must not go on strike and refuse to work until the boss relents to his demands as a member of a labor union. He must not join them after work at the bar and get a little drunk with a few beers or shots before going home. He must be spiritually different. He needs to remember who he is: a friend of God, a child of God's covenant, redeemed through the precious blood of Christ.

But his calling is not merely negative, not merely to keep himself unspotted from the world. He also has a positive calling to shine his light before men. That does not mean he has to preach to his coworkers every day that they are sinners on the path to hell and that they need to repent and turn to Christ. But it means he ought to listen, observe, and look for an opportunity to share the good news of salvation with those who are yet lost.

He must remember that he has been given the great treasure of Christ, the hope of eternal life in God's covenant, while that other man does not have Christ and is outside the covenant. But perhaps that man is now suffering. Perhaps he has major financial problems. Perhaps he is an alcoholic who is reaping what he has sown in his life. Perhaps his wife is about to leave him because of his bad behavior. Perhaps his loved one has recently been diagnosed with cancer or passed away. How do you react to that in your mind? We may be inclined to react by judging him for his bad behavior, or pitying him, but saying nothing. Let us rather view it as an opportunity to invite the man to lunch to tell him what God has done for us in Christ and to show him from Scripture the comfort of those who know Christ.

A man who is a friend of God must not form intimate friendships with his unbelieving neighbors either. The people of the world form friendships with each other on the basis of some common earthly interest such as sports. We ought not to form such superficial friendships, because friendship with the world is enmity with God (James 4:4). We ought not to get together with our unbelieving neighbors day after day for the sole purpose of watching the baseball or football game together. What does that amount to? If all we ever do with our neighbor is sit in the man cave with him for a few hours, jumping up to slap hands when our team scores, moaning and groaning when they are losing, drink a few beers and go home, that amounts to a pretty poor witness.

It is not wrong to watch sports once in a while. But it is a violation of our calling to come out from among the ungodly if we are forming friendships with unbelievers on the flimsy basis of a common interest in sports or any other earthly interest. If that is our only purpose with the relationship, we ought to come out of the neighbor's house and be separate.

But it is a very different thing when we seek to build rapport with our unbelieving neighbor with a view to inviting him to church. We may develop a relationship with him if our motive is love for him as a lost sinner and the desire to lead him to Christ. We may invite him to go out for coffee or even a beer if our purpose is to talk to him about the Christian faith. We may go over and watch that baseball game with him if we are consciously and intentionally looking for an opportunity to turn the conversation to spiritual things. We may invite him and his family into our home or onto our back deck for a meal if our desire is to witness to them by our Christian conduct and invite them eventually to attend a Bible study or a worship service to hear the gospel.

Perhaps we tend to think that no one is really interested in attending our church. The preaching is too deep. The sermon is too long. The worship is too formal. The songs are too hard to sing. But are *we* really interested in attending church either, by nature? We are just as interested in entertainment as the worldly man is, except for the grace of God. God may be giving the same grace to your neighbor, and he may intend to use your witness to draw him to the gospel. Take a little time to explain what your services are like and why your church does what it does. Then when the time comes, if they are interested, take them with you and help them through the service.

One more area of application regarding the covenant, antithesis, and missions, this time to young people. A young man or woman who is a friend of God ought not to date an unbeliever.[2] The people of the world date each other on the basis of sexual attraction or common earthly interests. But the children of God may not date on that basis and ought not to date someone of the world on that basis.

Dating is not evangelism. When I was a missionary in the Philippines, where the Christian young people often struggle to find other like-minded young people whom they might date, I was told about the common practice that they call in Filipino-English *evange-ligaw*, or evange-dating. Evangelizing plus dating equals evange-dating. The practice of dating is used not only to get to know someone with a view to marriage but also to evangelize unbelievers. This idea is no doubt mainly an excuse to date an unbeliever to whom one is attracted. As missionaries, we strongly discouraged that practice, and our spiritually mature Filipino brethren agreed that it was not a good practice. The Lord has made abundantly clear in Scripture that when the young men or women of the covenant marry the heathen, they are led astray into idolatry and unbelief (see Gen. 6:2; Deut. 7:3–4; Judges 3:6; 1 Cor. 7:39).

Dating must take place within the sphere of the covenant. That sphere does not include cults and false churches, such as

---

2 For a sound and balanced discussion of this point, see Joshua Engelsma, *Dating Differently: A Guide to Reformed Dating* (Jenison, MI: Reformed Free Publishing Association, 2019), 52–55.

the thousands of liberal churches that deny the cardinal doctrines of the Christian faith and teach whatever the secular culture dictates. On the other hand, the sphere of the covenant is not limited to just one denomination but includes all true churches of Jesus Christ that still have the candlestick of Christ's gospel. But since the candlestick burns more brightly in some churches than others, young people do well to look for a spouse within the churches that most faithfully preach the gospel, administer the sacraments, and exercise Christian discipline according to the Scriptures, so far as they can tell by the guidance of the Spirit who is in them.

They ought not to date or marry someone who is obviously just a nominal Christian, but who does not really know Christ. Nor ought they to compromise their convictions and leave a church where the candlestick of the gospel burns brightly and the Scriptures are taught faithfully in order to date and marry someone from a church where it burns less brightly. But they ought to date and marry within the sphere of the covenant and strive to make sure that the person is like-minded in his or her love for Christ and godly walk of life.

Dating is not evangelism. When it comes to dating, we must maintain the antithesis, come out from among them, and be separate. What do we do, then, when we are attracted to a person who is not a believer? We resist the desire to start a romantic relationship with them and make clear that we will not date them unless God leads them to become a committed Christian. We witness to them, if they are willing to hear, concerning Jesus Christ our Lord and what it means to follow him. We guard our heart with all diligence so that we maintain a posture of witnessing before ever even cherishing the hope of dating the person. And we pray for God to help us and guide us.

GO INTO ALL THE WORLD, BUT BE YE SEPARATE

We all struggle and fail in this area of the Christian life. I do too, all the time. I often do not know what to say to my neighbors or how to say it. I often fight against the fear of their rejection or ridicule that keeps my lips silent.

But we must remember who we are and what God calls us to be in this world. We are the people of God, the friends of God, through Jesus Christ our Lord. Therefore, we must walk as such, spiritually different from the world but also doing our best to show Christ to that world. We should not think that there is any conflict between keeping ourselves unspotted from the world and seeking contact with the people of the world to witness to them. Rather, let us think of it this way: we ought to live in antithesis to the world *by witnessing to the world*. Let us carry our candles in the darkness by speech that shows our hope and joy in Christ.

STUDY QUESTIONS

1. How do you harmonize the callings to "come out of the world and live separately as God's covenant people" and to "go into the world and shine as lights"?

2. What are the pros and cons of living in a Reformed "ghetto" (a neighborhood that is almost entirely made up of conservative Christians)?

3. What are some ways you could interact with your neighbors in order to bring them the gospel without violating the command to be separate from the world?

4. Do successful marriages in which one person dated another into the church prove that dating can be an effective form of evangelism? Why or why not?

7

GO INTO ALL THE WORLD, BUT FEED MY SHEEP!

When the doctrines of the antithesis and the covenant with us and our children are emphatically taught for a long time, but the call to evangelize the lost is rarely taught and hardly ever emphasized, it can result in a separatist mindset in the church. This can affect ministers too, and the way we think about our ministers. We know that Jesus said we must go into all the world and teach all nations. But did he not also call us to feed his sheep and lambs? Indeed he did (John 21:15–17).

Yet sometimes our focus betrays the belief that our calling is only toward the sheep within the fold and not also toward the sheep lost in the darkness (Luke 15:4). We leaders understand that we are watchmen on the walls of Zion who are called to defend the city and attack the enemy, but we forget our equally important calling to go outside the gates of the city and tell others of the wonderful works of God in Christ with speech that is always with grace and seasoned with salt (Col. 4:6). When this separatist thinking characterizes an entire church community, it should be no surprise if the ministers have little zeal for missions.

An Ingrown Church

In a paper entitled "Structure for Domestic Missions," Wilbur Bruinsma borrows a phrase from Presbyterian pastor C. John Miller's book *Outgrowing the Ingrown Church*.[1] Bruinsma writes:

> The best word to describe the consequences of a church that is interested almost exclusively in self and that lacks mission zeal is "ingrown." An ingrown church is that denomination of churches that has turned in on itself. Its clergy and membership focus the vast majority of their attention on the affairs of their own denomination without paying much attention to what is going on around them, except in a critical way.[2]

I am talking here about an ingrown church: a church that focuses most of her attention on her own affairs and people and devotes little attention to reaching the world beyond her walls; a church that believes the world is her mortal enemy but forgets that it is also a field throughout which Christ sows the wheat seeds of his elect through the witness of the church, or a sea into which the church must cast her net to gather all kinds into the kingdom of heaven (Matt. 13:38, 47).

Many of us who are pastors in small, conservative Reformed or Presbyterian denominations might recognize this as a more or less accurate description of our own churches. If we are

---

[1] C. John Miller, *Outgrowing the Ingrown Church* (Grand Rapids, MI: Zondervan, 1999).

[2] Wilbur Bruinsma, "Structure for Domestic Missions" (unpublished syllabus, 2011), 19.

honest, many of us will have to admit that we devote the lion's share of our thoughts, prayers, energies, resources, and conversations to the means God uses to continue his covenant with us and our seed after us, and a much smaller share to the means God uses to extend his covenant with those outside the church. The focus is on the need to pastor the young and old members of the covenantal community of which we are a part. The focus is on the many vacant churches that need a pastor and the many Christian schools that need teachers. The prayers go up for these needs, as they should, since we must pray to the Lord of the harvest to send forth laborers. We pray, too, for the seminary, where we expect professors of theology to train men to be good preachers, counselors, and churchmen who will be useful within the denomination. Mind you, I am not belittling or criticizing any of this, but only pointing out where our focus tends to lie.

In all this intense focus on the needs of our own churches, schools, and homes, we tend to forget about missions. We raise up our little boys and girls to think that the greatest need in the church is always for more pastors for the churches and teachers for the schools, but not so much for more missionaries to send out into the world. Thus we perpetuate a church culture that lacks fervent attention to missions and that is to some degree separatist. We might call it "an Old Testament church culture." Jon Mahtani expressed that idea when he wrote:

> An insightful elder once observed not so articulately, "Rev, I think sometimes our view of the covenant is Old Testament." There is some truth to that. We live in the New Testament age where there is supposed to be an emphasis on the gathering of others into the covenant, but we live

focused like the Jewish people mainly on God's covenant with our generations.[3]

In such a church culture, the ecclesiastical assemblies (consistory, classis, and synod) are often consumed with putting out the flames of one controversy after another in the endeavor to keep the unity of the Spirit in the bond of peace (Eph. 4:3). Speaking of controversies, Bruinsma makes the point that an ingrown church that does not repent of leaving her first love begins to spiral downward. He quotes Miller:

> In the introverted church we find that the members use their tongues a great deal—not to witness or pray or praise or to affirm one another, but to publicly review one another's flaws, doings, and sins...But why is this so?...Unbelief and fear characterizes the mental outlook in the ingrown church...There is often a failure to cultivate among leaders and people a spirit of forgiveness, mutual forbearance, and love. In brief, there is a shortage of real love in the congregation, a love fueled by a faith that has rejected the temptation to gossip.[4]

Bruinsma adds his own thoughts:

> The church that places little stress on sharing the gospel with others becomes suspicious, critical, and judgmental of others. It begins with an attitude of haughtiness toward all those outside of the borders of their denomination.

---

3 Mahtani, "Evangelistic Character of the Covenant," 452.
4 Cecil John Miller, *Outgrowing the Ingrown Church* (Grand Rapids, MI: Zondervan Publishing House, 1986), 33–34.

> The clergy and members of the ingrown church place their churches on a pedestal viewing themselves as the sole guardian of the truth. Instead of zealously sharing with others what God has given them, they hoard the gospel and look down on all others.[5]

Thus the ingrown church that insulates itself from the world, rather than reaching out actively to the world in evangelism, tends to multiply controversy after controversy. There is fear of heresy, suspicion of ministers, and a hypercritical attitude that is justified as necessary, lest we compromise our doctrine in a single jot or tittle. This is a seedbed for bitterness, judgmentalism, and envy, which are obviously some of the poisonous ingredients of polarization and schism.

When such a mentality develops in a covenantal community, the members cannot expect God to raise up young men who are full of joyful zeal for his mission to bring the gospel to the whole world. When we are only praying for pastors for our churches and teachers for our schools, we cannot expect God to raise up many men who are willing to leave behind their families and friends, cross cultural boundaries, live in poor and dangerous places, learn new languages, eat strange foods, and become all things to all men on a mission field. We should rather expect that God will give us men who have the same separatist mentality as the churches, men who are products of the ingrown mindset, men with little interest or vision for missions.

---

5 Bruinsma, "Structure," 22.

GO INTO ALL THE WORLD

The Gift of Missionaries

However, it does not have to be like that in the church. The church can be brought to see that it must outgrow its ingrown mindset. The church can be brought to adjust its focus from inward to outward until a better balance is achieved. The church can be convinced, by the enlightening power of the Holy Spirit and through biblical arguments, that she is indeed a city on a hill that cannot be hid, a light that must shine into the world, an institution with the calling to pastor the sheep within *and* seek the lost sheep outside her walls.

Then she will find that her head swivels back and forth, looking inward and outward, in a constant effort to assign the proper amount of attention to the established church and to those who will soon be brought out of the world into the covenantal community. She will not be at ease in Zion, enjoying her pleasant and prosperous life and claiming that her mission efforts are the best she can do. But she will be constantly in prayer for God to raise up more missionaries whom she can send and open more fields where they can preach.

When the church balances its focus so that it gives equal attention to going into the world with the gospel and feeding the sheep who are already within the fold, God will raise up more men who are zealous to be missionaries. In the churches of which I am a member, it has often taken a long time for a minister to accept a call to missionary service abroad. I am not judging anyone who has declined a call to the mission field. I once declined a call to a mission field in the Philippines before the Lord later brought me to accept the call a year later.

But one cannot help but wonder if we would see more men accept calls to mission fields if the churches as a whole were more mission-minded, if the families were more supportive and zealous for missions, if the schools were promoting missions. We must never expect every man who receives a call to missions to accept that call. God gives different gifts to different men and applies the great commission to our hearts differently too. But we can hope and pray that more men will accept calls to be missionaries than we have seen in the past.

I have heard it said that God raises up one man to be a Paul, and another to be a Timothy. A man like Paul is one who is not only theologically stalwart and pastorally wise, but who also longs to preach the gospel out in the world, even in places where Christ has not yet been named (Rom. 15:20). A man like Timothy is one who will "abide still at Ephesus" (1 Tim. 1:3), a man who will stay in a local established church, pastoring the flock, training future pastors, and doing the work of evangelism in the community around him. Most of us pastors begin our ministry in an established church. We are like Timothy in that way. But when we receive a call to be a missionary, God confronts us with the question whether we have the gifts and zeal to be a Paul, to bring the gospel outside the church, even to people who know nothing about Christ.

When a covenantal community is heavily focused on her own needs, we cannot expect there to be many, if any, ministers with the kind of gifts and burden that Paul had. I may be wrong, but it seems to me that when most of the members of a church are at ease in Zion, enjoying the "good life" of North America, we cannot expect men to rise up out of their midst with the willingness to preach the gospel to the heathen, at the risk of losing their lives. But when we repent of our carnal thinking and focus more and more by faith on the heavenly and eternal kingdom, we will grow in our sense of the urgency of missions. Then we may also see men step forward, prepared by God's grace from their mother's womb and throughout their childhood, who are ready to go into all the world with the gospel, come what may.

What a joy it would be if the Lord would open the door to more fields of labor, whether near or far, and give us ministers who count it a privilege to go into the world and preach the glad tidings. How wonderful it would be if Christ would provide more men with the gifts and zeal to teach the Reformed faith where only the Roman Catholic or Arminian Christ has been named. What a cause for thanksgiving to God if he gave us men with the gifts and zeal to go to the frontier of missions, to enter a strange culture, lower their standard of living, and study the local language in order better to reach heathen men and women who have never heard the gospel.

Perhaps you say: "Our denomination is too small to do much mission work out in the world." We have too few churches, members, and ministers, or perhaps too many vacant congregations that need a pastor. But what did God say to Gideon? "The people that are with thee are too many for me to give the Midianites into their hands" (Judges 7:2). Let us believe that God can do great things with small numbers. We need to be good stewards of the resources we have. But we also need to be bold and brave in pressing forward with the work of the Lord in missions, whatever amount of resources we might have.

The Missionary in the World

When a minister accepts a call to a mission field, having become convinced in his heart that Christ is sending him to go into the world to preach his gospel, that man must remain spiritually distinct from the world.

GO INTO ALL THE WORLD, BUT FEED MY SHEEP

The missionary is a man of the covenant. He has been called out of darkness into a relationship of fellowship and friendship with God through the Spirit of Jesus Christ. He has been baptized, as a sign of that covenant, in the name of the Father, Son, and Holy Ghost, either as an infant or as an adult. He has been taught, probably from childhood up, about the wretchedness of his sins and the God whose Son died to establish a covenant of grace with him. He has been admitted through profession of his faith into the Christian church as a confessing member. He has participated in the Lord's supper in the assembly of the saints, eating the broken bread and drinking the wine that symbolizes the blood of the new covenant. He has learned to walk with God and with his brothers and sisters in Christ in joyful gratitude by striving to keep the commandments of the covenant. In short, he has walked with God by faith for some time already, for a missionary may not be a novice (1 Tim. 3:6).

Now God calls him to go outside that covenantal community and labor as a missionary somewhere in the world. Thus, he must go *into* the world but remain spiritually *separate* from that world in the way he lives. He must be resolved, now more than ever, by the grace of God, to live as a man of the covenant, as he plunges into the darkness. He leaves the fellowship and accountability of the covenantal community and enters the domain where darkness holds unbroken sway. Notice a few things about this.

First, this does not mean that the missionary must maintain all the customs of his own church on the mission field, and even impose them on new converts. In fact, he must have wisdom from above to evaluate what is black, white, and gray even more carefully than when he was still in his home church. He must have a firm resolve to do what is right and teach it to the people with whom he labors. But he must also be open and flexible to adapt to customs that are different from what he is familiar with. My wife and I would sometimes remind ourselves when we were in the Philippines that our American customs were not necessarily better than those of the Filipinos. Different does not always mean better. If we think that our ways are always better than theirs, we are probably infected with some cultural and spiritual pride.

We must remember what Paul wrote: "I made myself servant unto all, that I might gain the more. And unto the Jews I became as a Jew, that I might gain the Jews…To them that are without law [Gentiles], as without law…that I might gain them that are without law. To the weak became I as weak, that I might gain the weak: I am made all things to all men, that I might by all means save some" (1 Cor. 9:19–22). The driving motive of the missionary is *by all means* to save some sinners, to the glory of God. The missionary understands that Christ was in the form of God but took on the form of a servant and humbled himself unto death for the missionary's own personal salvation. Therefore, he is willing to lose the comfortable life he once enjoyed, to whatever degree and for however long a time, in order to be used by Christ to gain others into the covenant.

The missionary must be willing to *adapt*. He must be willing to carry out his ministry in a very different context. He might wear different kinds of clothing in church than he did back home. He might eat different kinds of food at different times of day than he is used to. He might choose to have only one car, even though it might be more convenient to have two, in order to lessen the standard of living gap between him and people on the mission field who have much less. He might adjust his thinking about what it means to be "on time" or "late" for a meeting, or whether the most important thing is to accomplish a goal efficiently or to keep good relationships in good condition.

He might tolerate or even embrace different kinds of musical accompaniment in the worship services. He might learn the mother tongue of the native people and use it in his ministry. He might even construct his sermons a little differently, with inductive rather than deductive reasoning, with simpler language and sentence structure, or with illustrations from daily life in that mission field. In short, the missionary must become all things to all men within the clear boundaries of God's law in order to avoid spoiling the Lord's work of bringing others to salvation.

But second, the missionary must live the Christian life in an exemplary way on the mission field (1 Tim. 3:1-7; Titus 1:5-9). He must keep himself unspotted from the world. He goes into the realm of Satan where evil reigns, idols stand tall in their temples, and the lies of the serpent run wild and free. He must not drink the cup of the Lord and the cup of devils.

He must remember that even though he may be far away from his home church, family, and friends, God still sees everything he does. God sees the unfaithful missionary drinking too much alcohol in the hazy tavern with the drunkards, greedily stuffing his fat belly in front of the poor, sexually abusing a woman or child, sitting at the gambling table with fools, dancing with the ungodly to the beat of wicked music. God calls the missionary to put off anger, wrath, and malice not just back home but all the more on the mission field. God calls him to guard his tongue from cursing and swearing, boasting and bragging. God calls him to crucify any pride or haughtiness toward those he deems inferior to him. Oh what damage is done to Christianity and the honor of God by the missionary who is supposed to represent the glorious covenant of God but who acts like the heathen and joins in the darkness! The life of the missionary must be antithetical to what was just described.

The faithful missionary is a man who has a personal relationship with the God of the covenant. He has tasted the goodness of God in Christ, and he finds it sweeter than honey and more precious than gold, better than all the pleasures that intoxicate the hearts of men. He knows that Christ died for him. He experiences the blessedness of the forgiveness of sins by faith in Christ. He has real fellowship with God by faith day by day. He enters the sanctuary of prayer morning, noon, and night to worship and ask God for the things that he knows he needs. He runs with patience the race that is set before him, striving to lay aside every weight and the sin that so easily besets him, looking to Jesus the author and finisher of his faith (Heb. 12:2). He seeks to cultivate love for his neighbor, even for his enemies, and to forgive those who have sinned against him.

When God prepares a man to be a foreign missionary, God gives him a willingness to sacrifice the comforts of home, family, and friends and to count all things loss for the excellency of knowing Christ and making him known afar off. God works in him the resolve to be content in an unfamiliar place with a harsher climate, heavier traffic, a less developed infrastructure, a culture gap between him and the people, and even persecution. God moves him to seek strength in the midst of the struggles of mission life from heaven above and to drink deeply from the fountain of divine grace each day through prayer. God leads him to contemplate the cross of Christ and marvel at it as the most wonderful thing he has ever seen, which takes his breath away over and over. That amazing cross guards his soul from fastening on the illusions of happiness that are the empty things of the world.

Third, the missionary of the covenant must also preach the gospel of the covenant, a message that is antithetical to the lies of the world. He must preach the message that Jehovah alone is God, the creator of the universe who dwells in covenant within himself as Father, Son, and Holy Spirit, and there is no other god beside him. That message is distinct and bold in a world that worships a pantheon of gods and detests the exclusive claims of Christianity. He must preach the unpopular message that we are all corrupt sinners in Adam, conceived and born totally depraved by nature. Then he must also preach the gospel that there is no other name under heaven whereby we must be saved than the name of Jesus, the promised Messiah, the Mediator of the covenant, who because of his death and resurrection is the only Way for sinners to inherit eternal life. That message is also scandalous in a world of men who seek salvation in other names, who scoff at the cross, and who pray to saints, angels, and spirits.

The missionary must preach the message that God establishes an everlasting covenant of grace with all whom he predestinated to eternal life. That message of unconditional election will also incite opposition from a world that worships the doctrine of man's free will. The message must emphasize that God does not establish his covenant with men on the condition that they do something first, but God brings men into his covenant by sovereign grace and gives them faith whereby they enjoy a foretaste of fellowship with God in this life.

The missionary must preach the call of the gospel, which is also antithetical in nature. In a world that rushes headlong toward the damnation of hell, the missionary must utter from the housetops: "Repent, and turn from idols to the living God." He must preach the warning of the gospel that those who continue in sin and reject the gospel will be damned. He must preach the promise of the gospel that those who come to the Light and believe the gospel will be saved. Although the promise of the covenant is particular, the proclamation of that promise must be general. "Believe in the Lord Jesus Christ," the missionary must cry out, "and thou shalt be saved into the everlasting covenant in which God will be your God and dwell with you forever."

Finally, the missionary must teach believers all the antithetical commands of Christ. "Follow Christ," he must say, "by keeping all his commandments in gratitude for what he has done for you." When the missionary himself is practicing what he preaches, living an antithetical and thankful life on the mission field, his exhortations will carry more weight and be more effective. He must call converts to live the life of the covenant, the life of thankfulness to their God who called them out of darkness into his marvelous light. He must patiently disciple them in all aspects of the Christian life and call them to be transformed from their former conduct to the Christian life by the renewing of their minds.

May God raise up and send out many men as heralds of his covenant in the world.

GO INTO ALL THE WORLD, BUT FEED MY SHEEP

STUDY QUESTIONS

1. What is an ingrown church? Why is that a bad thing? How can a congregation or denomination outgrow being that kind of church?

2. Does a church have to be more mission-minded for there to be more missionaries, or do there have to be more missionaries for a church to become more mission-minded?

3. After reading what this chapter says about "the missionary in the world," list some practical ways a missionary could adapt to the foreign culture in which he lives. List some of the ways he can be flexible as he teaches on a mission field. List some of the things about which he must be strict and rigid.

FINDING MOTIVATION TO EVANGELIZE FROM GOD'S COVENANT

In his little book, *Evangelism in the Established Church*, Jason Kortering listed nine mentalities that hinder personal evangelism and argued against them. Among them was the argument that goes like this:

> Is not our emphasis on the covenant an obstacle to personal evangelism? We emphasize correctly the importance of the Christian home, the Christian church, and the Christian day school. This makes us introspective and self-focused as people of God. If we do this in obedience to Christ, how are we supposed to reach out to others who do not share this view and who even reject it? Won't we lose our covenant perspective?[1]

---

1 Jason L. Kortering, *Evangelism in the Established Church: The Calling of Committees and Individuals Concerning the Work of Evangelism* (Grand Rapids, MI: Evangelism Committee of First PRC, repr. March 2012), 41.

Those who think of the covenant primarily, if not exclusively, in terms of the promise of God to us and our children may fall into this lopsided way of thinking. But I will argue in this chapter that a proper understanding and embracing of the covenant of grace actually enlarges the heart of the Christian and motivates him or her to desire the salvation of lost sinners around us, and thus to be busy in personal evangelism. The question we face in this chapter is: what is our motivation as missionaries, pastors, and Christians to reach out to the lost and bring them the gospel, especially in this day and age when there is growing hostility to Christianity? The answer, I will argue, lies in the blessed reality of God's everlasting covenant with us in Christ.

Why the Lack of Motivation?

Are we motivated to engage in personal evangelism, to tell lost souls how Christ saved *our* lost souls, or do we lack motivation and ignore opportunities even when they stare us in the face? If we are honest, we will all admit that we often lack motivation to talk about God with unbelievers. There are surely a number of explanations for this. Probably we don't want to risk creating an uncomfortable or awkward situation. What if my neighbor mocks me or criticizes what I say? What if he embarrasses me by asking hard questions that I don't know how to answer? What if I accidentally say something wrong?

We all need to remember the reassuring words of our Lord: "Blessed are they which are persecuted for righteousness' sake: for theirs is the kingdom of heaven…Rejoice, and be exceeding glad: for great is your reward in heaven: for so persecuted they the prophets which were before you" (Matt. 5:10–12). And this:

"Take no thought how or what ye shall speak: for it shall be given you in that same hour what ye shall speak. For it is not ye that speak, but the Spirit of your Father which speaketh in you" (10:19–20).

But part of the explanation for a lack of motivation might be that we are too much at ease in Zion (Amos 6:1). Now it should be said, first, that it is not wrong to feel blessed when we seek to perform the duties of our station and calling as members of the covenant of grace. When we marry within the sphere of the covenant, bring children into this world, and present them for baptism; when we train up our little ones in the way that they should go and strive to fulfill the demands of the covenant in the home, work, school, and church; God blesses us. It is written: "Blessed is everyone that feareth the LORD; that walketh in his ways…happy shalt thou be, and it shall be well with thee. Thy wife shall be as a fruitful vine by the sides of thine house: thy children like olive plants round about thy table. Behold, that thus shall the man be blessed that feareth the LORD" (Ps. 128:1–3).

Nevertheless, we are too much at ease in Zion if we make no effort to show the salvation of the Lord to those outside the church. That is, if we do not care to be a witness to our neighbors, we show that we are spiritually complacent regarding the great work of God extending his covenant to the ends of the earth. We are too satisfied with our comfortable life inside the confines of the covenantal community. We are too silent about the wonderful works of God when we interact with people outside the church. There is something wrong in our hearts if we feel no motivation to talk about God with our neighbor.

That lack of motivation is a lack of love for God and for our neighbor. That lack of love is not unique to unbelievers. We are guilty of it, too, if we have little desire to "show forth

[Jehovah's] salvation from day to day" (Ps. 96:2) to sinners who are on the path that leads to damnation; or if we have little desire to "declare [Jehovah's] glory among the heathen, his wonders among all people" (v. 3). If all we are really motivated to do is make more and more money, get the most pleasure out of life, and make sure that our kids get a good education so they, too, can succeed, then we act no differently than the ungodly around us. They, too, have a natural love for their children and strive to ensure their success. We act differently than the ungodly when we teach our children to put God first in their lives, to live as pilgrims and strangers in the earth, and to witness to the lost with the desire that they come to Christ, if God wills.

I believe that when God-fearing people pour very little energy into personal evangelism, one of the culprits may be an underdeveloped or lopsided view of the covenant. The church is an "enabler" of complacency regarding missions when she only speaks of the *covenant* in terms of believers and their seed in the lines of continued generations, and only speaks of the *world* as that realm of darkness from which we must remain separate. She enables her members to think that they are living faithfully as God's covenantal people if they raise their children in the fear of the Lord, even if they never say a word about the Lord to their neighbors. The church must not enable believers to be complacent regarding their witness to the world. The church must exhort us constantly, in the words of Christ, not to hide our light under a bushel but to let it shine before men.

What does the covenant of grace motivate us to do? It certainly motivates us to walk with God in our personal life. It absolutely motivates us to raise our children in the nurture and admonition of the Lord. When we know that we and our children are members of the covenant of grace together, we are motivated to be busy in the work of Christian parenting, piously and religiously educating our children to the best of our ability.

We treasure the promise of God to continue his covenant with our children after us in their generations. We recoil at the thought of God visiting the iniquity of the fathers upon the children to the third and fourth generation, the thought of God cutting us off in our generations. We are motivated to train our children thoroughly in the faith of our fathers that we may show "to the generation to come the praises of the Lord, and his strength, and his wonderful works that he hath done" (Ps. 78:4).

But we will also be motivated to evangelize when we understand the covenant properly and embrace it warmly. The covenant is something much bigger than us and our children. The covenant embraces the whole creation, stretching back to the garden of Eden and forward to the new heavens and earth, stretching from the east to the west and all throughout the nations, extending to men and women from all nations and walks of life.

When we grasp that, we will be motivated to be busy in the work of evangelism. We will not think of a covenantal emphasis as an *obstacle* to personal evangelism. But we will see that the grand covenantal purpose of God *drives* us into personal evangelism because God will use our witness to bring outsiders into his covenant. What a joy it must have been for Paul to say to the Ephesians:

> 11. Wherefore remember, that ye being in time past Gentiles in the flesh, who are called Uncircumcision by

that which is called the Circumcision in the flesh made by hands;
12. That at that time ye were without Christ, being aliens from the commonwealth of Israel, and strangers from the covenants of promise, having no hope, and without God in the world:
13. But now in Christ Jesus ye who sometimes were far off are made nigh by the blood of Christ. (Eph. 2:11–13)

How Does the Covenant Motivate Us to Witness?

What is the covenant? Is it *the promise* of God to us and our children? *The sacrament* of baptism applied to the infants of believers? *The pact* of God with believers and their seed? *The procedure* by which God saves his people in the lines of the generations of believers and their children? *The duty* of Christian parents to raise their children in the fear of the Lord? If the covenant is defined in any of those ways, I do not see how it could ever motivate us to evangelize the lost. What comes to your mind when you hear the word *covenant*?

What comes to my mind is the relationship of close friendship and fellowship that the holy God of all creation has freely established with me, an unworthy sinner, through the cross of Jesus Christ and by the work of the Holy Spirit. We are unworthy sinners in ourselves, just like all the lost sinners who live around us. In Ezekiel 16, God inspired his prophet to describe Israel as a poor baby girl, unwanted and cast aside at birth, lying polluted in her own blood. That's what we were by nature: filthy, unlovely, and lost, indeed the very enemies of God.

But as we lay there alone and pitiful in the puddle of our own blood, utterly unable to save ourselves and plummeting toward the bottomless pit of death and hell, God said to us: "Live!" He said: "When I passed by thee, and looked upon thee, behold, thy time was the time of love; and I spread my skirt over thee, and covered thy nakedness; yea, I sware unto thee, and entered into a covenant with thee, saith the Lord God, and thou becamest mine" (Ezek. 16:8).

God covered our nakedness and washed away our filthiness through his own Son, whom he sent to descend into that bottomless pit of death and hell in our place on the cross. Every time we celebrate the Lord's supper, our souls sing for joy as we drink the cup of wine and remember the promise of Christ: "This is my blood of the new covenant which is shed for many for the remission of sins" (Matt. 26:28). Christ took our sins upon himself and suffered the punishment in our place on the cross to remove the enmity between us and God, to reconcile us to God, and to confirm the new and everlasting covenant of grace with us once and for all.

Christ now comes to us in our lives through the person of the Holy Spirit and enters into that covenant with us by uniting us to himself and dwelling in our hearts. He gives us the gift of faith, so that we know God through Christ as our God and begin to experience a little of what it means to be in a relationship of closest friendship with him.

That is what the covenant of God is: the relationship of intimate fellowship that the sovereign God establishes with us through Christ, the bond of love in which he embraces us as his sons and daughters, as members of his one big family that includes men and women from the whole human race. The covenant is the relationship of sweet communion that God establishes with me, maintains with me, and will perfect with me, and not with me only, but also with all those whom he has chosen and redeemed in Christ. The covenant is that everlasting life that God has given and will give to me whom he has saved, merely of grace, only for the sake of Christ. The covenant will never end, but it is the very essence of the blessedness of salvation. The covenant formula in Scripture, the phrase that appears again and again and defines the nature of the covenant, is that God is our God and we are his people.

Do we grasp that in our hearts? God's love for us is so great that he wills to dwell with us for all eternity in intimate fellowship, that he will never leave us or forsake us, that he will keep us as the apple of his eye so that we have nothing to fear in life or death, and that he desires to commune with us face to face through Christ throughout the long ages of eternity! If we truly understand and appreciate how good God has been to us to draw us into his everlasting covenant of grace through Christ, then we will be motivated to open our lips and bear witness to our glorious God! The Holy Spirit kindles a fire of devotion in the hearts of those who know God as their everlasting God in Christ, so that they go forth and speak of "the wonderful works of God" (Acts 2:11).

What is the Christian motivated to do in his life? Deep down, the thankful believer longs to glorify God in all that he does. We glorify God when we praise his name in prayer and song, in the home and at church on Sunday. We glorify God when we avoid profanity and swearing in the workplace. But we glorify God in a special way when we declare his glory among the heathen, when we confess his name before the world, when we let our light shine before men.

When we pray "hallowed be thy name," we are asking God to work in our lives so that we glorify him in respect to all his wondrous works and live our lives in such a way that his name is never blasphemed because of us but rather honored and praised.[2] God has created us as a people for himself to show forth his praises in the world (Isa. 43:21; 1 Pet. 2:9). Are we not motivated to glorify God by showing forth his praises and thus shining as lights in a world of darkness?

Bringing Outsiders into the Covenantal Community

As members of the covenant of grace, think of all the many wonderful blessings we enjoy within our community of believers: the beautiful preaching of the gospel and participation in the holy sacraments as food and drink for our hungry and thirsty souls from Sunday to Sunday; the amazing benefit of catechetical instruction in the riches of the word of God from our childhood through our youth; a Christian education that teaches us about God in connection with every area of human knowledge and experience. We are members of a church family in which we benefit from the spiritual gifts of the other members and enjoy the blessings of Christian love, friendship, and fellowship with those of like precious faith. We can find a spouse who believes in the same Christ and values the same heavenly treasures that we do and then raise a family in a stable environment with the rhythms of worship, work, study, and fellowship. The list goes on and on when it comes to the blessings of life in the covenant.

The ultimate goals of missions and evangelism are to convert the elect among the heathen to Christ and lead them and their families to become members of the church of Christ for the glory of God. When we feel comfortable within our

---

2 Heidelberg Catechism Q&A 122, in *Confessions and Church Order*, 136–137.

covenantal community, we can lack the desire to bring others into it from the outside. Outsiders might change the dynamics of our church. They might be rough around the edges. They might not fit into our church culture. What if they do not wear the same kind of church clothes that we wear? What if they do things on the Lord's Day that we consider out of bounds for a Christian? What if they are a danger to our congregation? The list of what-if questions is endless.

Many what-if questions are important ones. But some of them reveal our selfishness, legalism, excessive fear, or lack of true love for our neighbor. If our congregation is made up of believers from one main ethnic group (for example, Dutch American) and several extended family units, it might feel disturbing, almost like an invasion, if several outsiders start attending. What if they take over the church? What if they change the direction of the church? What if they corrupt the doctrine?

But instead of thinking like that, we should be thinking of our blessed heritage as something that we want others to have too. I think we are driven by fear far too often when it comes to evangelism. We think we are justified and reasonable with our fears and worries. But God tells us not to fear but to trust him and obey. He has given us an inestimable treasure, an unspeakable gift, by establishing his covenant with us in Christ. He promises to give these covenantal blessings to our elect children after us in the lines of continued generations.

But he also promises to give them to his elect children who are still in the world, whom he has decreed to bring into the covenant, perhaps through your witness. Who are we to stand in the way of God's decree if one of those people is rough around the edges? Rather, we ought to have a real desire in our hearts that many would come to Christ and join our congregation, regardless of their ethnicity or socioeconomic status. As Paul said to Herod Agrippa: "I would to God, that not only thou, but also all that hear me this day, were both almost, and altogether such as I am, except these bonds" (Acts 26:29).

In Reformed missions and evangelism, we do not seek merely the conversion of individuals to Christ, but also their incorporation into the church with their families. Daniel Kleyn, one of my former missionary colleagues in the Philippines, emphasizes this as a fundamental difference between Reformed and Arminian missions. He writes that "Arminian doctrine is *individualistic*, and thus their approach to missions is the same. But Reformed doctrine is *covenantal*, and thus the Reformed approach to missions is covenantal." He goes on to assert that "the Reformed church keeps in mind in its mission work the truth of God's covenant. That covenant has a bearing on missions, for God's covenant promise and purpose is to gather the elect, ordinarily, from the generations of believers and their seed…God, in His wisdom, wills to save, not simply individuals here and there, but families." Therefore, he concludes: "Families are the objects of our labor on the mission field. Our desire is that families gather under the preaching of the word. We see to it that not only parents and adults are instructed in the truth, but that the children are also instructed in it."[3]

We must not be timid about welcoming new people into our covenantal communities with their families. We should count it a great joy to disciple new families as they learn the doctrines and work through whatever problems and questions

---

3 Daniel Kleyn, "Reformed versus Arminian Missions (1): Different Objects," *Standard Bearer* 96, no. 8 (January 15, 2020): 188–189.

they will have brought along with them. We should be eager to share with them the wonderful benefits of life in the covenant that God has graciously given to us and our families. We should be delighted to help them learn the way we do things and why we do them that way, and to assure them that they do not have to look or be exactly the same as everyone else. We should be ready and willing to plug them into the life of the church, to get their children into the catechism classes, to invite them warmly to attend the Bible studies, to show hospitality to them in our homes, to give them a tour of the Christian schools, explain what a blessing they are, worth far more than the cost of the tuition, and answer their questions.

In his refutation of the mentality that thinks our covenantal perspective hinders evangelism, Jason Kortering writes:

> The covenant emphasis that we enjoy, on the basis of the Bible, is that we walk with our God in every activity. This marks us as Christian, and we will not compromise our convictions of faith and practice…The reason for our joyful walk of faith in every circumstance, in prosperity and adversity, is our God and His love for us. If we take this approach, our covenantal blessings will not deter us from reaching out or tempt us to abandon them, but rather encourage us to appreciate these blessings and be ready to share them with others. Again, we cannot prejudge whether others will care about it, respond appreciatively, or mock us. This is in God's hands. One thing is for sure, we don't have to hold back because of our faith and understanding of God's covenant. As Reformed believers, our goal is not simply to "save souls" but to bring souls into God's covenant, including the church, home,

and school...What a thrill it is when others receive eyes to see and hearts to believe such a wonderful truth. The evidence of grace is that they quickly learn to appreciate this covenant life.[4]

STUDY QUESTIONS

1. How does a correct understanding of the covenant motivate us to be busier with world missions and local evangelism?

2. Are you uncomfortable with the idea of bringing outsiders of different ethnic groups or socio-economic levels into your congregation? If so, why?

3. What can you do to help invite new members or families into the life of your congregation or Christian school?

---

4 Kortering, *Evangelism*, 41–42.

9

EVANGELIZING IN HOPE OF THE FINAL PERFECTION OF GOD'S COVENANT

When God directs our attention to the future, to the end of the world, he reveals his will regarding the culmination of his covenant and the end of our mission to the world. In biblical eschatology, we see these two great themes of Holy Scripture, the covenant and missions, converging at a single point. The covenant will not be perfected at some point in history *before* we have finished our mission to the world. But the covenant will reach perfection and carry us into the kingdom that God has prepared for us from the foundation of the world at the very point when our mission has been completed: the end of the age when Christ will suddenly appear in power and great glory on the clouds of heaven. This part of Scripture is the content of our Christian hope, and I believe there is something worth exploring here about the covenant and missions.

In the Scriptures that contain the most noteworthy prophecies of the end of the world, we are struck by a remarkable connection between the perfection of God's covenant and the completion of the church's mission to the world. Jesus taught very clearly that the completion of the church's mission will mark the end of the world. He told his disciples in the Olivet Discourse: "And this gospel of the kingdom shall be preached in all the world for a witness unto all nations; and then shall the end come" (Matt. 24:14; Mark 13:10).

Jesus did not mean merely, as many postmillennialists teach, that there would be a preaching of the gospel in all the Mediterranean world within one generation after his death, and then the destruction of Jerusalem would take place, so that this prophecy has already been entirely fulfilled in the past. Nor did he mean, as many premillennialists explain him, that there will be a special preaching of the gospel in all the world after God raptures the church out of the world, so that this prophecy will be entirely fulfilled in a future age after we Christians are gone.

No, the meaning of this prophecy of our Lord is that the preaching of the gospel will go into all the world and bear witness to the truth among all nations throughout the entirety of this present age; and when it has reached everyone whom God has ordained it to reach, the end of the world will come. While Christ certainly had in mind all the preaching that would take place *within* the covenantal community to us who would be born and raised in the church and continue as members of the church until our dying day, his focus is nevertheless on the preaching that would take place *outside* the covenantal community in the great field of the world. Christ has called us to go into all the world and preach the gospel to every creature and make disciples in all nations, and he promised that when this task is finished, the end of the world will come. When this task is finished, he shall return on the clouds of heaven with power and great glory and send his angels to gather his elect from one end of heaven to the other (Matt. 24:30–31).

EVANGELIZING IN HOPE OF THE FINAL PERFECTION

That moment will also mark the culmination and perfection of the covenant of grace. John saw in one of his last visions that after Christ returns, destroys the beast and the false prophet, and judges all men from his great white throne, there will be "a new heaven and a new earth: for the first heaven and the first earth were passed away" (Rev. 21:1). John says: "I John saw the holy city, new Jerusalem, coming down from God out of heaven, prepared as a bride adorned for her husband" (v. 2). The old Jerusalem was the city at the center of the covenantal community of the nation of Israel in the Old Testament. But the new Jerusalem is the name of the whole covenantal community of the elect from all nations that is also known as the church, the Bride of Christ.

John sees her adorned for her husband, perfectly prepared for her wedding day, for the beginning of her everlasting life with Christ. Then he says these marvelous words that foretell the perfection of the covenant of grace:

3. And I heard a great voice out of heaven saying, Behold, the tabernacle of God is with men, and he will dwell with them, and they shall be his people, and God himself shall be with them, and be their God.
4. And God shall wipe away all tears from their eyes; and there shall be no more death, neither sorrow, nor crying, neither shall there be any more pain: for the former things are passed away. (Rev. 21:3–4)

The tabernacle in the Old Testament was the holy tent that was erected in the midst of Israel in the wilderness as a symbol of God's dwelling with his people in covenantal fellowship. But the tabernacle that John saw in a vision is Christ, the Word become flesh to dwell among us in the closest fellowship possible between God and man for all eternity (John 1:14). John saw God dwelling with men, with his elect people from all nations and ages of history, in intimate covenantal fellowship. "He will dwell with them, and they shall be his people, and God himself shall be with them, and be their God" (Rev. 21:3). That is the sweet covenantal formula that runs like a golden thread through the Scriptures and reaches its majestic crescendo in this vision of the eternal age to come. These are the simple but wondrous words that reveal the essential nature of the covenant of God with men.

God will dwell with us. We will be his people. He will be with us. He will be our God. What John sees here is the perfection of the covenant in the new heaven and earth that God will create when Christ returns. What he sees is the everlasting blessedness that will be experienced by all who come to Christ when God draws them by his word and Spirit.

Thus the themes of the covenant and missions converge at the end of the world. There is an important connection between them that we must see, a connection that will increase our zeal for missions and spur us to be busy in evangelism when we do see it. The establishment of the covenant with the elect in Christ does not merely run on the track of the generations of us believers and our seed, but it also flows in the same riverbed as the progress of missions, and it will do so until the end of time. The two prophecies we considered above, when we understand them together, teach us that the glorious perfection of God's covenant will not take place until we finish our mission to the world.

That does not mean that the perfection of the covenant *depends* on us finishing our mission in all nations. Not at all! God depends on no one but himself for the realization of all his decrees. But what it means is that the perfection of the covenant will take place *through* our completion of the mission Christ has given us. God has ordained that he will bring his covenant to glorious heights of everlasting perfection in the new creation *after* he has established it with people in every nation, tribe, and tongue through the mission work and evangelism that he calls us to do.

That is a powerful motivator to be active in missions and evangelism! Does it not motivate you to put forth greater effort, to strive with greater energy, in personal, congregational, domestic, and foreign missions? Let us not strangle the hopeful motivation that these truths are meant to give us by the negative mindset that expects small things, few converts, little progress.

Jesus once taught a parable about a mustard seed. He said: "The kingdom of heaven is like to a grain of mustard seed, which a man took, and sowed in his field: which indeed is the least of all seeds: but when it is grown, it is the greatest among herbs, and becometh a tree, so that the birds of the air come and lodge in the branches thereof" (Matt. 13:31–32). Jesus did not mean that the kingdom of God would start small but eventually overtake all the kingdoms of this world *within history* and become the greatest of all kingdoms *here on earth*. No, the mustard seed of the kingdom of God will grow into the greatest of all herbs and become a tree *in the world to come*. But that being said, Jesus intends to fill our hearts with hope through this parable, that although the kingdom of God always appears very small and weak in this world, *it will grow* into a great tree. We must not be pessimistic about our mission efforts, as if they will never amount to anything.

Thus we must not focus in an unhealthy way on prophecies of apostasy and lawlessness that we see being fulfilled right before our eyes in the world today. We do need to pay attention to the signs of Christ's coming, including those of apostasy and increasing iniquity in the world (2 Thess. 2:3; Matt. 24:12). But we ought to guard ourselves against thinking that we know the hour of the Lord's return with a growing degree of certainty and accuracy, that it must be only a few months or years away. Sometimes we talk that way. We see the falling away of many and the unraveling of a once more or less Christian society, and we assume that the end of the world must be only a few years hence. But we must remember that we do not know the day or hour of Christ's return. We do not know if he will come in a few years or a hundred years or more.

Remember that many of the great reformers of the sixteenth century thought they were living in the last years of history. Surely the falling away of the church in the Middle Ages was the great apostasy! Surely the world could not get any worse than the way it was in Europe in the 1500s! But five hundred more years have passed since then.

In the meantime, massive missionary efforts have taken place in the "new world" that was discovered through exploration, and large numbers of people have been drawn to Christ in the heathen world. The nineteenth century has come to be known as the great century of missions. But the twentieth century also saw tremendous developments in world missions. In this twenty-first century, we do not know how far away the end is. What we know is that Christ calls us to keep running the race of evangelization until we cross the finish line.

What we are doing when we reach out to the lost, whether in the secular West, the Islamic Middle East, or the pagan nations of the Orient, is not a labor that is vain and futile, even when we see few converts. We have a blessed and great hope before us. We have the hope that through our labors, our missions, our witness to the world, God will establish his covenant with all whom he has ordained to eternal life, one by one, family by family, nation by nation, until he has reached every last one of his people with the gospel and brought them to a saving faith in Jesus.

Jesus taught another parable along with the parable of the mustard seed. He said: "The kingdom of heaven is like unto leaven, which a woman took, and hid in three measures of meal, till the whole was leavened" (Matt. 13:33). He gives us hope through these parables that through our evangelistic endeavors God is working in the world, causing the kingdom of heaven to permeate like yeast through the dough of the nations, and bringing the world closer and closer to the end he has determined for it. We have the hope that in this way God will certainly raise up his covenant to that height of glory that he showed to John in a vision.

We reach out to the lost in hope of the final perfection of God's covenant. Hope drives us forward. Hope gives us energy. Hope keeps us going. We may not slow down. We must keep running the race. We must keep sending missionaries. The covenant is being established, maintained, and perfected more and more as we draw nearer and nearer to the end.

What a glorious day it will be when our mission is completed and we arrive with all God's people on the shores of eternity to dwell with God, our God, in sweet communion forever! What a day it will be when we see Jesus face to face, the Jesus who sent us on our mission, and walk and talk with God in the flesh! May that day come quickly. Let us pick up the pace of fulfilling our mission until it does.

STUDY QUESTIONS

1. How do the themes of covenant and mission converge at the end of the world?

2. Do the biblical prophecies of a future apostasy and tribulation mean we should not expect great things from mission work in the present?

3. How can hope for the final perfection of God's covenant drive us to be busier in our mission efforts?

Appendix 1

THE GREAT COMMISSION

"Go ye therefore, and teach all nations, baptizing them in the name of the Father, and of the Son, and of the Holy Ghost: Teaching them to observe all things whatsoever I have commanded you: and, lo, I am with you always, even unto the end of the world. Amen." —*Matthew 28:19-20*

"Go ye into all the world, and preach the gospel to every creature." —*Mark 16:15*

Here we are. Gathered around the feet of the Master, high up in a mountain of Galilee, where the view of the sea, hills, and fields below is truly spectacular. Only recently our Lord and Savior arose from the dead and showed himself to us by many infallible proofs, by which we are now sure that his love covered our sins and conquered death on the cross. Oh, the joy to see our beloved Savior again before he goes up in the cloud to sit at the right hand of the Majesty on high!

Our Lord has a final word for us. Something urgent and of worldwide significance. Some new command and commission. What a breathtaking location for this final word! For here we can look panoramically at the whole world, to the east, to the north, to the south, to the west.

Now listen, he is about to speak. "Go ye," says our all-powerful and exalted Master, "into all the world and teach all nations. Preach the gospel…Baptize those who believe…Teach them to observe all things…And lo, I am with you always."

Go.

Simple, yet demanding task! It is simple enough to understand the call to go, for every day we are going somewhere, from one place to another. But so demanding! For he is calling us to go out of our sphere of familiarity, our beloved life here in Galilee near that little sea down there, and into all those nations of the world!

Oh, but let us now recall that he himself went out from his realm of heavenly splendor, being sent by the Father, and came into this world to save us poor lost sinners from our sins and the destruction we deserve. Is it such a great thing, then, if we his disciples are to follow in his footsteps? Indeed, remember what he told us not long ago, that as his Father sent him, even so he is sending us.

For that matter, has he ever told us that the way would be easy? Was it easy for him to go into the world and suffer reproach and forsakenness and death? Demanding is this mission from our God that calls us to leave our comfort zone, our earthly home, our families and friends, and go to nations and places afar off, where the customs and language are strange to us and the people sometimes hostile. But looking up into the face of the Lord and hearing the urgency of his tone, we know that he means what he says with utmost seriousness.

Go!

Into all nations of the world! Did he not direct us once to go only to the lost sheep of the house of Israel? Yes, but remember how our brethren according to the flesh have despised and rejected him, crying out for his crucifixion! Do you remember how he said to us that many shall come from the east and west and shall sit down with Abraham, and Isaac, and Jacob, in the kingdom of heaven?

The time has come, brethren, for the ingathering of the Gentiles, the fulfillment of the promise to father Abraham that in him all the families of the earth would be blessed. Into all the world! For he taught us that God so loved the world that he gave his only begotten Son that all who believe in him should not perish but have everlasting life. The sheep must be found and drawn to the Shepherd. The gospel of the kingdom must be preached in all the world—so he told us on the Mount of Olives—for a witness unto all nations, and then shall the end come, the glorious appearing of the Master on the clouds of heaven!

So we go! To Jew and Gentile, high and low, rich and poor, male and female, dark- and light-skinned. We are runners, brethren, with a glorious torch to carry into all the world! We must press toward the mark, not slowing down as we draw near to the finish line, but pushing ourselves to run faster and harder, into all nations.

What an amazing privilege he has just given to us, his specially called and ordained apostles! To be leaders in his church whom he will use to build his church upon the rock of brother Peter's confession that Jesus is the Christ, the Son of the living God! We are no men of high repute or earthly power, no kings or governors, whom he has sent to do this task, but mere servants of our King, in a spiritual kingdom, ordained ministers of the gospel.

What a blessed work we are sent to do, and not only we, but *all* whom the Master calls into this ministry of the word, laborers in his vineyard, pastors and teachers in his church, preachers of the gospel of peace and glad tidings of good things! Let *all* who follow after us do the work of an evangelist. Let them go out into the highways and byways and bid their neighbors to the marriage of the Lord. Let them not be ashamed of the gospel of Christ but be eager and open and ready to speak with their lost, heathen neighbors. Let them go, too, into other nations, across vast oceans, over mighty mountains, afar off to preach the gospel or aid and encourage those who do.

And oh, that *all* his disciples—male and female, farmer, sailor, builder, lawyer, doctor, engineer, craftsman, businessman, single and married, mother and father—would support and participate in our great commission! Oh, that they all would pray for us, with intimate understanding of our work, that the word of the Lord may have free course and be glorified. Oh, that they would give cheerfully and liberally to support us who preach the gospel so that we need not make tents or have another occupation to eat our daily bread. Oh, that they might have opportunity to visit us on faraway mission fields to witness the glorious work and appreciate it all the more.

But oh, that they would themselves participate, being ready always to give an answer to everyone who asks them a reason for the hope that is in them! Oh, that they would shine as lights in the world, in the midst of crooked and perverse nations, ready and eager to hold forth the word of life to those who are without. Not ashamed of the gospel of Christ, but knowing that it is the power of God unto salvation to everyone who believes. Would to God that they would radiate every day with the hope of eternal life, having faces that show that the joy of the Lord is their strength. Master, use them, too, to bring others into the fold to hear the blessed tidings of salvation! Give them, too, to hear the call—Go!—as the Lord puts in front of them an opportunity in their daily life to bear witness of Christ Jesus.

Go…and teach.

That's what the Master said. "Make disciples" is what he told us to do. Simple, yet highly demanding task! Surely he does not mean *we* can make anyone into a disciple of the living God, but that he will do so through us. But still, is not a disciple one who both believes in our Lord and Savior and follows him in all areas of his life, through thick and thin, even at the cost of losing his life? We will need to have tremendous patience in this task. We will need to be committed to those who show vital interest in the gospel. We will need to have a long view of things.

But what a blessed task is ours. For the Lord has seen fit to make disciples in all nations by sending us to preach the gospel! To declare that he came into the world to save sinners. To herald that he must have suffered on the cross and given his life a ransom for many to redeem us from the curse of the law. To make known that he arose from the dead for our justification. To speak of the breadth, length, depth, and height of the love of Christ for us whom God has chosen before the foundation of the world. To speak of the glories of everlasting life with God in a world without end for all who love the appearing of the Master on the clouds on that great and notable day of the Lord!

Baptizing them…

What a joy that will be when men and women are drawn by the Father and given true faith in Jesus through the power of the Holy Spirit so that they may be baptized into his triune name! What a moving experience it will be to apply the waters of baptism to those sheep who are as yet still afar off! To give them this new sacrament, this holy sign and seal, which bespeaks their union with the triune God and their inclusion in the eternal family: God the Father witnessing unto them that he makes an eternal covenant of grace with them and adopts them to be his children and heirs; God the Son promising them that he has washed away all their sins by his precious blood; and God the Holy Ghost sealing unto them that he dwells in them and will sanctify them more and more.

What a wonder our Lord is revealing unto us, that the Lord of hosts, the God of our fathers, is indeed one God but in three persons, a Father with his Son in loving communion through the Holy Spirit. And what an awesome blessing that he is drawing us and all who believe and we are baptized into his divine life! Believers, and their seed. For our God has always extended the promise to us and our children, and our Lord told us to let the children come to him and forbid them not. So we will baptize these believers with all their household, and new lines of the covenant promise will begin!

Teaching them to observe…

The Lord has still more for us to do. Our task will not yet be complete when the heathen are converted to Christ and baptized. But what a joy it is, too, to teach! All things that thou hast taught us, Lord? Thou hast taught us so much. The gospel of the kingdom of God! The precepts of thy kingdom—love, forgiveness, compassion, humility, meekness, faithfulness, generosity, truth, courage, conviction, spirituality, trust, and doing all things to the glory of God. There is much to teach, so we must get busy and make disciples who know all thy doctrines and who strive to follow all thy precepts with delight.

But Lord, this commission is greater than we.

Lo, I am with you always, even unto the end of the age. You are not alone, but I am with you. When you stand up to preach to the multitudes, I will be with you. When you are driven out of town, shackled up in prison, lying under a pile of stones, I am with you. When words fail you and strength is gone, I will not leave you. When you leave father and mother, sister and brother, and go to faraway places, I will go with you. I will be with you always. I will never leave you or forsake you. I will bless your lips so you may give an answer to those who ask a reason of the hope that is in you, with meekness and fear. Do you believe that I am with you? Believe this promise with all your heart, and go! *There will never be a time until the very end of this present age, until I return on the clouds of heaven, as I am about to go, when I will not be with you. For you are my servants whom I love, and I intend to use you for the coming of my kingdom.*

So go, in this confidence.
Into all the world!
Until I come again.

Appendix 2

ECHOING THE WORD

In her book *Say Among the Heathen the Lord Reigns*, Jean Kortering tells the conversion stories of several individuals in the continent of Asia. The first story is about a young girl in Singapore named Poh Li who was raised by a strict Buddhist mother and a father who was a gambler and drunkard. One day, a young woman named Karen of the Covenant Evangelical Reformed Church saw Poh Li in a store studying a picture of Jesus. Karen asked her if she knew who was in that picture, and Poh Li said no. So Karen started to tell her about Jesus and asked if she would like to learn more. Poh Li said yes, and they began to meet.

Karen eventually invited her to church, and she began coming and hearing the preaching of the gospel through Pastor Jason Kortering. But Poh Li's mother was not happy about it and would cane her legs when she came home from church. The girl persevered even when she could not come to church for a time, and she grew in her faith.

Several years later, the Korterings saw her again. She excitedly told them that both her parents, to whom she had faithfully witnessed, had repented of their pagan beliefs and ungodly ways and become Christians.

Karen did not know and certainly did not expect that the Lord would use her simple little remark to kindle a flame in Poh Li's heart and that later the flame would be spread abroad into the lives of so many others. It is God's work alone that calls his children out of darkness into his marvelous light, but there are means through which he works. May we all be faithful witnesses of the glorious truth that he has revealed to us in his word.[1]

Has the gospel come to you not in word only but also in power, in the Holy Ghost, and in much assurance (1 Thess. 1:5)? Have you become a follower of the apostles and missionaries and an example to other believers by your sounding out the word of the Lord, not only in your local area but everywhere your faith in God is spread abroad (vv. 6–8)? That was true of the Christians of Thessalonica in Macedonia. They appear in Scripture as marvelous examples of the personal evangelism that is the calling of us all. They show forth the relationship between official preaching of the gospel and the unofficial witness of all believers.

The official preaching of the gospel is the chief means God uses to save the lost. Although the preaching of the gospel comes to mankind through mere earthen vessels, "that the excellency of the power may be of God, and not of us" (2 Cor. 4:7), it is "the power of God unto salvation to everyone that believeth; to the Jew first, and also to the Greek" (Rom. 1:16). "For the preaching of the cross is to them that perish foolishness; but unto us which are saved it is the power of God" (1 Cor. 1:18).

---

[1] Jean Kortering, *Say Among the Heathen the Lord Reigns: Evidences in Southeast Asia* (Jenison, MI: Reformed Free Publishing Association, 2022), 35.

God makes the preaching of the gospel a power unto salvation for all whom he has predestinated to eternal life out of every nation; for all whom he gave to Christ to redeem from sin and death by dying for their sins and rising again the third day. For God is pleased to give us salvation through *faith* in the Christ who died and rose again (Rom. 10:9–13), and God is pleased to work that faith in us through the *preaching* that sets forth Christ crucified and risen as the only way of salvation and through which Christ himself calls us to repent and believe on him (vv. 14–17).

But how shall a man preach except he be sent? Therefore, God calls certain men to devote their lives to preaching and sends them through the church with authority to preach the gospel, both within the church and outside among the heathen. Some preachers spend most of their lives preaching primarily within the church. Others spend most of their lives preaching primarily among the heathen. But even those who labor primarily within the church must "do the work of an evangelist" outside the church in their local area (2 Tim. 4:5).

In 2008, Pastor Arie DenHartog spoke at a missions conference sponsored by the Domestic Mission Committee of the PRCA, similar to the one at which the content of this appendix was delivered in May of 2023. DenHartog called us to pray for boldness for the preaching of the gospel as it goes forth in missions in a day when ungodliness worsens, apostasy runs rampant, and ignorance of Scripture is widespread. Jason Kortering also spoke at that conference. He called for special training in missions including the creation of a "culture for missions" in the churches so that the children and youth grow up understanding the importance of missions. Do we pastors agree, and if so, are we endeavoring to create this culture for missions by our teaching, exhorting, and example as local evangelists?

The preaching we pastors sound forth every Sunday comes not in word only but also in power if the believers who hear it follow our example and sound forth that word wherever they go to the unchurched, as opportunity arises. That was what the Thessalonian Christians were doing. That was what Karen was doing when she responded to a young girl in a store studying a picture of Jesus by telling her about Jesus. Do you do that kind of thing?

The phrase "sounded out" in 1 Thessalonians 1:8 could be translated "echoed." They were echoing the word of the Lord everywhere they went. An echo is a unique sound because it is the repetition of an earlier sound. In a canyon, if you shout "hello," the sound wave goes out of your mouth, reflects off the wall of the canyon, bounces back to your ears, and you hear the echo of your own voice. When the apostle and others preached the word to the Thessalonians, the sweet sound of the gospel went out of their mouths and struck the hearts of the believers. When those believers went about their daily lives, that sweet sound reflected off their hearts and bounced outward, so that others heard the echo.

Like an echo, the sound that came out of them was the same sound they heard from the pulpit, the same word of the Lord. Unlike an echo, the repetition of that sound was not the automatic effect of a physical cause, but it was the result of a powerful, delightful, and mysterious spiritual cause. The Holy Spirit does not deal with us as he deals with the wall of a canyon that mindlessly echoes a sound. Rather, he sweetly bends our will so that we believe the gospel that we hear and our hearts are ignited with a flame of thankful joy in Christ. He sweetly moves our will so that we respond well when we hear our calling to share that gospel with others and we become eager to do so, according to our ability. He strengthens us with courage so that we are not afraid of what men may think of us and are not ashamed of the gospel, but we begin to echo it in our daily lives to our unbelieving neighbors.

When believers become faithful in echoing the word, as the Thessalonians were, their preacher may be able to exclaim: "We need not to speak anything!" (1 Thess. 1:8). In this comment of the apostle, we see not only the biblical warrant for zealous personal evangelizing by ordinary believers, but also the great effectiveness of such evangelizing. Mind you, this is the same apostle who teaches the primacy of preaching by ordained men as the power of God unto salvation. But here he rejoices in the echoing of that preaching by unordained men and women.

Let us not misunderstand. He was not throwing out the preaching, as if there was no more need for it in Macedonia. Rather, he was taking delight in the fact that the divine power at work in the preaching flowed like an electric current through ordinary believers, so that they, too, sounded out a witness everywhere they went, and consequently the apostles did not need to speak on every street corner or in every marketplace of Macedonia. God caused a little of the spiritual power that flows through faithful preaching to flow through the faithful echoing of that preaching as well.

How exactly does that work, or what exactly does that mean? Imagine for a moment that you are walking into a large stone church building somewhere in Europe. You immediately hear the echo of the most beautiful singing of a choir somewhere inside the building. You are not hearing the sound directly from the mouths of the singers, but after it has bounced off the walls and through the corridors of the building. You are captivated by that sound and drawn deeper into the building, down the hall, around the corner, because you want to hear the sound more clearly and fully and straight from the mouths of the singers.

In a similar way, God uses the echoing of his word by you unordained Christians. He goes before you to prepare the hearts of his elect who are lost in unbelief, so that when they hear you echo the preaching you heard in church, it captures their attention and draws them to hear the sweet sound of the gospel straight from the mouth of the ambassadors of Christ.

Therefore, the echoing of the word by ordinary believers is vitally important for the growth of the church and spread of the gospel. We preachers of the gospel must take the lead in fulfilling the great commission in the world and set an example by our own personal evangelizing in the places where we live. But we must spend most of our time in the study, reading our texts, exegeting the Scriptures, and crafting sermons to preach on the Lord's day. You members of the church, however, go forth into every nook and cranny of society in your daily lives as mechanics, engineers, farmers, doctors, builders, mothers.

You must understand and embrace your calling, as you have opportunity and according to the gifts God has given to you, to confess Christ before men and echo the word of the Lord everywhere you go. If there is no echoing of the word by the members of the church in the world, the church might grow from within for a while, but it will become what some have called an "ingrown church."[2] God grant that our churches continue to develop a "culture for missions" so that through our zealous echoing of the word of the Lord, others may be gained to Christ and added to the church from the outside, even as many as the Lord our God shall call.

---

2   See chapter 7.

Practically, there are many ways to echo the word: publishing a magazine, making a podcast, writing a blog, distributing pamphlets, and more. But the most important way, I am still convinced, is personal and even face-to-face interaction with the neighbors in your life. I know that we often do not have great opportunities to speak to our neighbors about our faith. I know that many of our neighbors want us to keep our religion to ourselves.

But look for the man or woman who is *interested*, as Karen noticed Poh Li staring at that picture of Jesus, and do not fail to open your mouth to talk to him or her about Christ. Realize that you need not cast your pearls before the swine who shamelessly express their militant atheism or disdain for Christ, but you may pray for them and let God deal with them as he will. But when God shows you a person with some level of interest in Scripture or openness to hearing the Christian faith, do not fail to follow up and pursue the person with your Bible and a willingness to talk.

Let it be primarily positive at first, not an immediate harsh condemnation of all their errors, but a speaking of the wonderful works of God in Christ in whom we have hope and joy. Let the troubles of your neighbor (cancer, divorce, loneliness) be a point of departure to speak of the comfort that is in Christ alone. Once you have developed some rapport with the person, invite him to church and take him with you to hear the sweet sound from the mouthpiece of the Savior. Remember to pray for your neighbors, not only those who show interest, but also those who do not. May God be pleased to use you to gain others to Christ, and may God be praised through your echoing of his word.

SCRIPTURE INDEX

OLD TESTAMENT

Genesis
1:26–28	13
2:7	13
2:8	13
2:16–17	13
2:21–23	13
3:8	13
3:8–9	16
3:15	16, 22
3:20	18
6:1–6	19
6:2	95
6:8	19
6:17–20	19
9:8–10	21
9:8–17	22
9:25–27	21
12:1	23
12:3	86
15:6	27
15:17–18	24
17	60
17:4–5	26, 28, 36, 60, 61
17:7	7, 8, 24, 25, 28, 36, 41, 52, 60, 61

Exodus
29:45	41
29:45–46	8

Deuteronomy
6:7	52
7:1–7	85
7:3–4	95
7:6–8	29
33:28	85

Joshua
6:25	53

Judges
3:6	95
7:2	106

Ruth
4:13	53

Nehemiah
9:7	23

Psalms
22:27	30
25:14	8
67:3–4	30
72:9–11	30
78:4	119
93:3, 10	86
96:2	117–118
96:3	118
96:10	30
103:17–18	25

SCRIPTURE INDEX

127	75
127:4	75
127:5	75
128:1–3	117

Isaiah

2:2	87
2:2–4	31
19:23–25	31
41:8	8
42:6–7	31, 86
43:10	86
46:6–7	86

Jeremiah

31:31–34	8
31:33	41

Ezekiel

16:8	8, 121

Amos

6:1	117

Jonah

1:2	53

Micah

4:1–4	31

Zechariah

8:22	31

NEW TESTAMENT

Matthew

5:10–12	116
5:13–16	33, 88
5:14	91
5:14–15	89
5:16	91
8:10–12	33
8:11	54
10:5–6	32
10:19–10	117
10:37–38	58
10:33	135
10:31–32	133
13:38, 47	100
16:18	9
16:25	46
24:12	19, 134
24:14	8, 130
24:30–31	130
24:36–39	19
26:28	2, 8, 33, 28
28:18–20	35
28:19	9
28:19–20	137

Mark

13:10	130
14:24	2, 33
16:15	9, 137
16:15–16	35

Luke

2:10–11	31
2:29–32	32
12:8	8
15:14	99
22:20	33
24:47–48	35

John

1:14	132
1:29	33
3:16	33
3:16–17	47
3:17	46
5:30	40
6:38	40
8:12	91

SCRIPTURE INDEX

10:15–16	61
17:15	73
17:15–16	67
17:16	89
17:18	38, 47
17:20–21	61
20:21	38
21:15–17	99

Acts

2:11	122
2:38–39	35
2:39	7, 25, 50, 62
13:46–48	89
13:48	6
26:17–18	9
26:18	90
26:29	125

1 Corinthians

1:18	146
1:21–29	57
7:39	95
9:19–22	108

2 Corinthians

4:7	146
6:14–18	88
6:16–18	8
6:17	73, 84
6:18	41
8:9	46

Romans

1:16	146
4:11–13	26–27
8:30	35
9:4–5	89
10:9–13	147
10:14–17	147
10:15	9
12:1–2	88
15:20	105

Galatians

3:8–9	27
3:15–17	8
3:16	24
3:26–29	36
3:27–29	25
4:1–7	87
4:4–5	38, 47

Ephesians

2	70
2:1–10	70
2:11–13	119–120
2:12	51
2:12–19	71
2:14	87
2:39	51
3	70
3:6	71
4:3	102
4:11	3, 79
5:1–14	88

Colossians

1:20	20
2:4–10	88
4:6	99

Philippians

2:15–16	92
3:14	19

1 Thessalonians

1:5	146
1:8	149
1:6–8	146
1:8	9
4:11	92

SCRIPTURE INDEX

2 Thessalonians
2:3

1 Timothy
1:3	105
1:15	15
2:4	33
2:5–6	34
3:1–7	109
3:6	107

2 Timothy
4:5	3, 79, 147

Titus
1:5–9	109

1 Peter
2:9	123
3:20–21	20
4:1–4	88

1 John
2:15	88
4:14	20, 38, 47

Hebrews
2:16	31
12:1–2	19
12:2	110

James
1:27	88
4:4	93

Revelation
21:1	131
21:2	131
21:3	8, 41, 132
21:3–4	131

YOU MIGHT ALSO LIKE

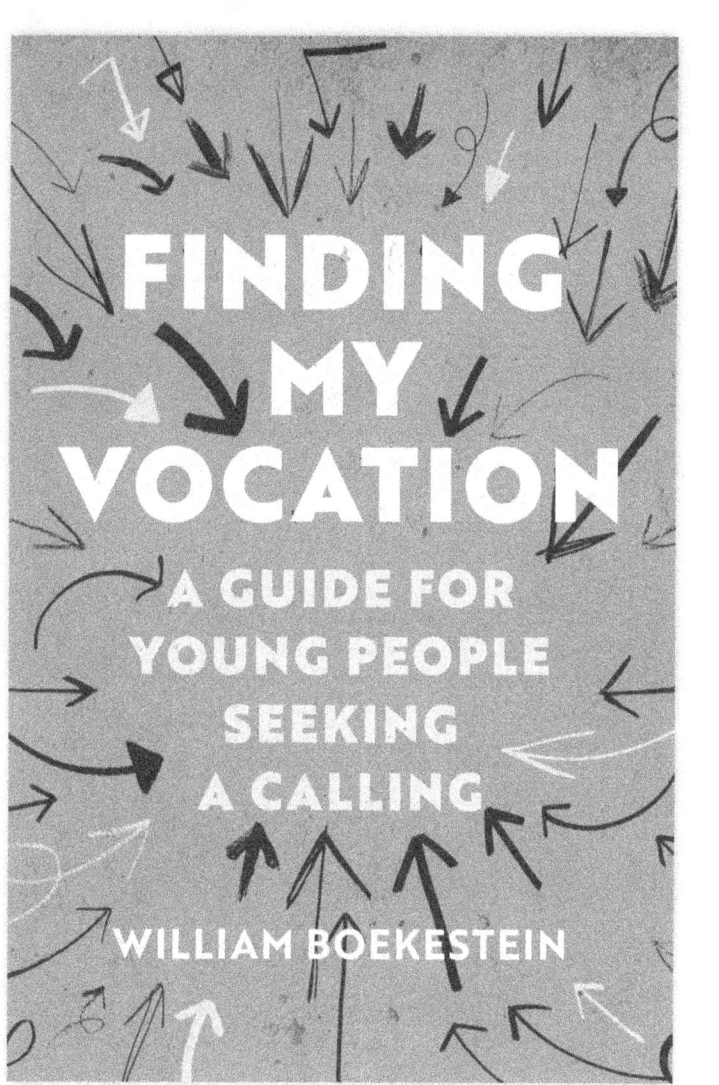

the FRUIT
love joy peace
of the SPIRIT
longsuffering gentleness goodness
of JESUS
faithfulness meekness temperance
CHRIST

Richard J. Smit

Life *in the* Covenant

in Family, Church, and World

Wilbur Bruinsma

Our Mission

To glorify God by making accessible to the broadest possible audience material that testifies to the truth of Scripture as understood and developed in the Reformed tradition.

Reformed Free Publishing Association
1894 Georgetown Center Drive, Jenison, MI 49428-7137
Website: rfpa.org
E-mail: mail@rfpa.org
Phone: 616-457-5970

www.ingramcontent.com/pod-product-compliance
Lightning Source LLC
Chambersburg PA
CBHW070539170426
43200CB00011B/2472

"Daniel Holstege has written an important book on the importance and necessity for every church to be engaged in outreach and evangelism. All churches would benefit from reading through, absorbing, and putting into practice what is here written."

—Paul T. Murphy, pastor of evangelism,
Messiah's Reformed Fellowship (New York)

"I read Daniel Holstege's book with appreciation and joy. He ably shows how the covenant of grace, even if one sees that covenant differently than him, should inspire us to preach the gospel to the nations. Too often we limit the covenant to discussions of parents and their children, when in fact the covenant is about that and so much more. The covenant demands that we also be outward-focused, preaching the gospel to those who are 'far off.' Holstege connects all these dots and urges Reformed churches to develop a culture of missions. Any Reformed reader (and beyond) would benefit from the well-researched and well-presented argument of this book."

—Eric Onderwater, pastor of Grace Canadian
Reformed Church (Brampton, Ontario)

"With a passion for both covenant theology and the great commission, Daniel Holstege offers a compelling call for churches to embrace their 'covenantal mission mandate.' Drawing from Scripture and the Reformed tradition, he challenges believers to see that God's covenant is not only for our children but also extends to the nations through the preaching of the gospel. Even where readers may differ on certain covenantal nuances, they will find this book to be a biblically grounded and stirring reminder that the church must proclaim Christ to all people, trusting that God will gather his own. A valuable and timely encouragement for those who long to see missions thrive in a covenantal framework."

—Tim Bergsma, pastor of Living Hope Free Reformed Church (Chatham, Ontario)

"Here is an important book on missions that is scriptural, doctrinal, practical, personal, and concise. What a unique and important work! God's people will be blessed as Daniel Holstege recounts his experiences as a missionary to the Philippines and his own personal development in love for the mission mandate of the church, all while carefully expounding that mandate for our benefit. Avoiding an imbalanced position, Rev. Holstege has developed a mature and holistic view of God's purposes that can be of great help to the church and the individual child of God. May God use it to grow many in love for him and the fullness of his covenant!"

—Cory J. Griess, Professor of Practical Theology and New Testament Studies, Protestant Reformed Theological Seminary (Wyoming, MI)